Gates of Excellence

Katherine Paterson

Gates of Excellence

ON READING AND WRITING

BOOKS FOR CHILDREN

LODESTAR BOOKS   DUTTON CHILDREN'S BOOKS   NEW YORK

Library of Congress Cataloging-in-Publication Data
Paterson, Katherine
Gates of excellence.
Summary: A collection of essays relating to the
author's experience as a writer of novels for children
and her ideas on children's literature in general.
1. Paterson, Katherine — Authorship — Addresses, essays,
lectures. 2. Children's literature — Authorship — Addresses,
essays, lectures. 3. Children — Books and reading — Addresses,
essays, lectures. [1. Paterson, Katherine —
Authorship — Addresses, essays, lectures. 2. Children's
literature — Authorship — Addresses, essays, lectures.
3. Children — Books and reading — Addresses, essays,
lectures] I. Title.
PS3566.A779Z465 1981 809'.89282 81-9698
ISBN 0-14-036225-8   AACR2

Published in the United States by Dutton Children's Books,
a division of Penguin Books USA Inc.

Editor: Virginia Buckley   Designer: Trish Parcell
Printed in the U.S.A.
10 9 8 7 6 5 4 3

1995 DOL 23224 10.00

ACKNOWLEDGMENTS

The author would like to acknowledge the following excerpts quoted in this book:

Page 3. Text from PEANUTS by Charles M. Schulz; © 1969 United Feature Syndicate, Inc.

Page 6. From *My Fair Lady*. Copyright © 1956 by Alan Jay Lerner & Frederick Loewe. Chappell & Co., Inc., owner of publication and allied rights throughout the world. International Copyright Secured. ALL RIGHTS RESERVED. Used by permission.

Page 56. Text from MISS PEACH by Mell Lazarus. Courtesy of Mell Lazarus and Field Newspaper Syndicate.

Page 113. From "Bridge Over Troubled Water" by Paul Simon; © 1969, 1970 Paul Simon. Used by permission.

For
Sara Little
and
George Parker Winship, Jr.

CONTENTS

❦

Gates of Excellence

BEFORE THE GATES OF EXCELLENCE

"Mrs. Paterson, when did you first know you wanted to be a writer?" My questioner was an intelligent, deeply serious young woman of eleven who had wanted all her life to be a writer. I was embarrassed to confess to her that I couldn't remember ever wanting to be a writer. At eleven, in fact, I was torn between a future as a foreign missionary and one as a movie star. The fantasy I acted out alone in the bottom of the backyard was as the leader of a commando unit that was single-handedly winning World War II. At night I often put myself to sleep with visions of the United States as a monarchy of which I was the brilliant and much-beloved queen.

Yet all those years I was writing. The works that survived the eighteen moves of my growing-up years are without exception terrible, at best dull, at the worst reeking with sentimentality. Perhaps the explanation for my lack of youthful literary ambition is that my critical faculties developed far earlier than my creative. I had been reading since I was five, and I am sure that I began to write not because of any ability real or imagined but because I loved to read, and that when I finally began to write books, it was not so much that I wanted to be a writer but that I loved books and wanted somehow to get inside the process, to have a part in their making.

By the time I got to college I had apparently read enough so that it was beginning to rub off a bit on my work. Indeed, an English professor once noted my chameleonic tendency to adopt the style of whatever literary figure I happened to be doing a paper on. I am grateful that he encouraged me to write papers on only the best. An apprenticeship imitating the masters of the English language was bound to have a beneficial effect.

In graduate school a favorite professor stopped me in the hall one day to ask if I had ever thought of becoming a writer. "No," I replied, swelling with twenty-four-year-old pomposity. "I wouldn't want to add another mediocre writer to the world." "But maybe that's what God is calling you to be." She meant, of course, that if I wasn't willing to risk mediocrity, I'd never accomplish anything, so when she recommended me eight years later for a professional curriculum writing assignment, I took the job. At the time I was pregnant with our first son and anxiously awaiting the arrival of our first daughter from a Hong Kong orphanage, but I said yes, and I've been writing steadily ever since.

I became a writer, then, in 1964 without ever really formulating the ambition to become one. When the curriculum assignment was completed, I turned to fiction, because that is what I most enjoy reading. By the fall of 1968 we had four children, a second son by the usual route and a second daughter by air from

Arizona, and I, writing in ten-minute cracks of time, was ready to begin my first novel.

I had no study in those days, not even a desk or file or bookcase to call mine alone. I was, I must admit, doing a lot of mediocre work, but with the encouragement, not to say nagging, of my husband, I was writing—learning and growing along with the children—until eventually I was writing fiction worthy of publication. It might have happened sooner had I had a room of my own and fewer children, but somehow I doubt it. For as I look back on what I have written, I can see that the very persons who have taken away my time and space are those who have given me something to say.

Now I have a study with bookcases, files, and an oversized wooden desk. Taped above the desk is a three-by-five card on which I have hand-printed a Greek saying that I borrowed from an Edith Hamilton book. In letters large enough to be read without my glasses, it says:

BEFORE THE GATES OF EXCELLENCE
THE HIGH GODS HAVE PLACED SWEAT

I always type with my back to it. Also out of my line of vision as I work is a *Peanuts* sequence that my typist in Maryland had mounted for me. Snoopy and typewriter are on the roof of the doghouse. "It," says the first frame. Then follow two frames of Snoopy pacing the roof. "It was"—pace. "It was a dark"—two more frames of pacing. "It was a dark and stormy night." In the final frame Snoopy looks up from the machine to observe: "Good writing is hard work."

They are both right, the Greek and the beagle. Even if in my terror of the specter of mediocrity I keep my back to them, I still

3

believe in the sweat theory of good writing. In addition, they serve to remind me that we writers are not a breed apart, a privileged aristocracy doling out gifts to less fortunate mortals, but rather that we are, like the majority of the human race, day laborers. And if we marvel at the artist who has written a great book, we must marvel more at those people whose lives are works of art and who don't even know it, who wouldn't believe it if they were told. However hard work good writing may be, it is easier than good living.

And finally, no matter how good the writing may be, a book is never complete until it is read. The writer does not pass through the gates of excellence alone, but in the company of readers. Most of my readers are young, storming the gates for a good story, always hopeful that the next book they pick up will be the best they have ever read. It is a joy to write fiction for such readers. I can't imagine, however, that they'd be curious about the person who writes for them. I certainly wouldn't have at their age. All I cared for was the novel itself.

But I have other readers, not all librarians or teachers, although many of them are, people whose senses are as keen as any artist's, who have learned and continue to learn how to see and hear and feel, and thus truly how to read. This book is my way of sharing with these my fellow laborers what it means in my life to be both reader and writer, struggling to pass through the gates of excellence.

WORDS

❧

When I told a friend of mine that I was going to tackle the subject of "words," she asked me quite naturally what I was going to say about them. "Well," I said, "I think I have something valid to say, I just haven't figured out what it is, yet." Which, of course, is one of the problems with words—there they all are—humanity's greatest natural resource, but most of us have trouble figuring out how to put them together in a valuable way.

So we blame it on the words. Words are cheap, we say. One picture is worth a thousand words. Silence is golden.

But words aren't cheap. They are very precious. They are like water, which gives life and growth and refreshment, but because it has always been abundant, we treat it cheaply. We waste it and pollute it and doctor it. Then, when we take a drink from a city faucet, we wrinkle our nose and say: "This is terrible water." And we blame the water because we have misused it.

Words, words, words [cries Eliza Doolittle]
I'm so sick of words.
I get words all day through
First from him, now from you.
Is that all you blighters can do?

Now there is probably not one of us who has not had the impulse in the middle of an interminable committee meeting to leap to his feet like Julie Andrews and sing out this protest, but as one of the blighters with a vested interest in the commodity, I feel the need from time to time to justify myself, especially to myself. I read the newspaper. I watch the eleven-o'clock news. I know as well as anyone else that the International Year of the Child came to an end with countless children starving to death in Cambodia. Children in Northern Ireland are still playing war—and not just pretend. My daily newspaper carries accounts of battered, even maimed, children in my own city. And this fall a six-year-old and a nine-year-old made a serious attempt to hold up a bank. The clerks thought it was cute.

And what am I doing while the world is falling apart? I am sitting in my little study in front of my typewriter trying to find words and put them together. Sometimes I see it as an evasion of responsibility, sometimes escape, and always as selfishness, since I particularly love what I'm doing. I'm uncomfortably reminded of the story of the old Quaker who, after his first cup of coffee, said: "Anything that tastes this good has got to be a sin."

But granted all this, still I believe that words, too, are necessities—and to give the children of the world the words they need is, in a real sense, to give them life and growth and refreshment.

Words

If sometimes today, I feel myself drowning in verbiage, I can remember clearly how it feels not to have any words. In those months after I went to Japan in 1957, I would often find myself being taken somewhere by Japanese friends, not knowing where I was going or whom I was going to see. When I got to wherever I had been taken, I would find myself surrounded by people who were talking and laughing away, but because I did not know their words, I was totally shut out. As I began to learn a few words, people would try with infinite, exaggerated patience to talk with me. And because my speech was so halting and miserable, they would try to help me, try to put words into my mouth, try to guess what on earth it was I was trying to convey. When I was finally able to get out a sentence near enough to Japanese so that my listeners could grasp what I was driving at, they felt sure I'd appreciate knowing how I *should* have expressed that particular thought, and they would gently, firmly, and ever so politely, take my pitiful little sentence apart and correct it for me.

I'm sorry to report that I was not grateful. I wanted to yell, cry, throw a tantrum. *I am not a fool!* I wanted to scream. If only you could know me in *English*, you would see at once what a clever, delightful person I am. But, of course, I didn't say it. I couldn't say it. I didn't have the minimum daily requirement in either vocabulary or syntax. The first time I saw the play *The Miracle Worker*, I knew what had been happening to me in those days. It was the rage of those starving for words.

In 1961, after four years in Japan, I boarded a jet in Tokyo and landed about twenty hours later in Baltimore. I was met by my parents and one of my sisters and taken home to Virginia. Every night for many weeks I would get out of the soft bed, which was killing my back, and lie sleepless on the floor. I was utterly miserable. "These people," I would say to myself, meaning my own family, "these people don't even know me." The reason I thought my family didn't know me was that they didn't know me in Japanese.

You see, in those four years I had become a different person. I had not only learned new ways to express myself, I had new thoughts to express. I had come by painful experience to a conclusion that linguists now advance: language is not simply the instrument by which we communicate thought. The language we speak will shape the thoughts and feelings themselves.

Because I remembered so well what it was like not to have words, it was easy for me to imagine, when I at last became a mother, what my children were going through when they were first learning to speak. In my great and just possibly superfluous concern I determined to help them all I could. I spoke to them from the first in complete English sentences, just as though they could take in every word I was saying. I read to them poems and wonderful books, far before an educator, indeed before any sensible person would think they could be ready to understand the words. But in the midst of this richness, when one of them would stand before me, the little cords straining in his neck, as he sought to express the still inexpressible, I would wait with totally uncharacteristic patience, reasoning that if they were to learn to speak freely and comfortably to me, I must be willing to listen. Nor would I correct their mistakes. It is rude, I thought, to correct the grammar of someone who is trying his best to tell you something, no matter how tall the person might happen to be. And if it was rude for me, it was certain to be frustrating and discouraging to the speaker. They would learn quite soon enough, I reasoned, the difference between the singular and plural form of the verb. All they had to do was listen. If not to me, to their father.

Well, the other day, the turkeys flew home to roost. One of them came home from school totally scandalized by a bit of information from his English teacher. "Do you know what she said?" he asked. And while I waited for the revelation of his teacher's radical political or moral philosophy, he continued in the same shocked tone: "She said I couldn't say, 'Who are you waiting for?' "

"She did?" I asked nervously.

"She said" —he could hardly believe it still— "she said I had to say, 'For whoooooom are you waiting?' "

"I'm afraid she's right."

"Whaaaaat? You think I'm going around saying 'For whoooom are you waiting?' Everybody would think I'd gone nuts."

The grammar lesson was obviously overdue. "No," I agreed. "If you went around saying 'For whooooooom are you waiting?' or even if I had a kid in a book who said, 'For whom are you waiting?' everyone would think we had taken leave of our senses, but, actually, your teacher is right. The correct, formal English is: 'For whom are you waiting?' "

He gave me a look of utter disgust and muttered "For whoom" several times under his breath, making it sound for all the world like an obscenity. Finally he said, "Why do we have to have proper grammar anyway? Why can't we just go around grunting like the cavemen?"

Now for all my failures as a teacher of English, I want to assure you that my son is not going to give up language and return to grunting. This is the child of ours so in need of language that, perceiving great lacks in English, he invents language and vocabulary to fill the gaps. There is, he perceived no adequate mild expletive in English. The Japanese have a very nice one—*Ara!*—but he didn't know Japanese. So he invented *bip*. When, for example, you are reading the newspaper and pouring yourself a glass of milk at the same time, and your mother suggests that you may have missed the glass, you can stop, look at the table, and say *bip*. A few years ago he invented *labysan*, which is harder to decode than pig Latin and has the added attraction that no one over the age of ten (except him) can possibly pronounce it.

In other words, he is a genuine human being with the very human drive for language. We humans have had from time unknown the compulsion to name things and thus to be able to deal with them. The name we give to something shapes our attitude toward it. And in ancient thought the name itself has power, so that to know someone's name is to have a certain power over him. And in some societies, as you know, there was a public name and a real or secret name, which would not be revealed to others.

Now the animals communicate with one another. They give signals of danger or mating calls. But they do not, as far as we know, name things. Jacob Bronowski says that an animal cry is a sentence, whereas in human language we have somehow miraculously broken down sentences into words—words that name objects and actions, which means then we can take these same words and rearrange them, reconstitute them into other sentences with quite different meanings. Because we name, we name ourselves, and we can think of ourselves as separate creatures, apart from nature. We can, therefore, using our vision and our power to create language, develop science and art.

But in this process of naming, of being able to take apart

nature, to study it, to communicate about it, in the very process that becomes our glory lies an insoluble paradox. And that is this: nature is intricately and infinitely connected. The minute I name something and begin to regard it as a separate entity, I break this unbreakable unity. So that which makes it possible for us to seek truths about the universe and about ourselves has within itself the guarantee that we will never be able to find the Truth. Our knowledge must be forever fragmented, because that is the nature of systematic knowledge.

"The world," and I am quoting now, "the world is totally connected. Whatever explanation we invent at any moment is a partial connection and its richness derives from the richness of such connections as we are able to make. . . . The act of imagination is the opening of the system so that it shows new connections."[1]

But what has all this esoteric talk about language and imagination to do with me—much less with you and why we are all together today?

I find the connection in a very disturbing essay by Joan Didion, entitled *Slouching Towards Bethlehem*. Didion wrote this essay at a time in 1967 when, in her own words, she felt forced to deal "directly and flatly with the evidence of atomization, the proof that things fall apart. I went," she says further, "to San Francisco because I had not been able to work in some months, had been paralyzed by the conviction that writing was an irrelevant act, that the world as I had understood it no longer existed. If I was to work again at all, it would be necessary for me to come to terms with disorder."

So Didion went to Haight-Ashbury to live for a while among

[1]Jacob Bronowski, *The Origins of Knowledge and Imagination* (New Haven: Yale University Press, 1978), p. 109.

the flower children. In her essay she piles up story after story of the children she meets—the flower children so glorified by the media but whom she regards in a much more somber light.

"We were seeing," Didion concludes, "the desperate attempt of a handful of pathetically unequipped children to create a community in a social vacuum. . . . These were the children who grew up cut loose from the web of cousins and great-aunts and family doctors and lifelong neighbors who had traditionally suggested and enforced the society's values. They are children who have moved around a lot. . . . They are less in rebellion against society than ignorant of it, able only to feed back certain of its most publicized self-doubts, *Vietnam, Saran-Wrap, diet pills, the Bomb.*

"They feed back exactly what is given them. Because they do not believe in words . . . and a thought that needs words is just one more of those ego trips—their only proficient vocabulary is in the society's platitudes. As it happens," and here at last Didion makes her own connection as well as the one I am trying to make today, "as it happens I am still committed to the idea that the ability to think for one's self depends upon one's mastery of the language, and I am not optimistic about children who will settle for saying, to indicate that their mother and father do not live together, that they come from 'a broken home.' They are sixteen, fifteen, fourteen years old, younger all the time, an army of children waiting to be given the words."[2]

Now this essay was written in 1967. No one is worried about the Flower Children of Haight-Ashbury anymore. They have long since, in a word of our times, "self-destructed."

But there are still children in 1979 waiting to be given the

[2]Joan Didion, *Slouching Towards Bethlehem* (New York: Delta Books–Dell Pub. Co., Inc., 1968), pp. 122–123.

words. I was talking recently to a woman who has the unenviable job of teaching young teenagers to read. These children are characteristically (in the non-word of one expert) "un-verbal." That is, their only proficient vocabulary is in obscenities and other current clichés. And if they are not at home with the spoken language, they are positively at war with the written word. The teacher described for me the anguish of these young people as they try to decode a single sentence. "We have wonderful books," she went on to say. "All designed to help them, to entice them to read. But they won't even open them."

Why won't they open them?

"Because they are books. And these children hate books."

I was in no position to make suggestions. I have always loved books passionately. I, who would never have made the gifted-and-talented program, still taught myself to read, simply because I loved books so much. I have noticed that the fact that I have no right to make a suggestion doesn't necessarily keep me from making one. But in this case, I was a little hesitant. The suggestion I wanted to make was such an obvious one. "Do you read aloud to them?" I asked.

She shook her head sadly. "Sometimes I do. A little. A short section or a paragraph, trying to interest them in something, but the administration frowns on it. They think I'd be simply entertaining these kids when they ought to be working."

I wanted to cry. We both wanted to cry. How can these children ever learn to read—why should they ever *want* to learn to read if books are enemies to be fought rather than friends who will enrich and broaden and give joy to their lives?

Then I told her about my friend Eddie. And at the risk of bragging, I'm going to tell you about Eddie because he seems to sum up what I'm trying to say and do.

Last spring I had been asked to speak in a junior high school, and I gave those in charge my usual little speech about what I would do and what I expected them to do. For example: I do not sing, dance or do card tricks, therefore, I will not attempt to entertain an auditorium full of bored children. I will speak to a classroom-sized group of students who have read something that I have written and who want to talk with me about it. I don't care a bit if they liked what they read or not, simply that it aroused sufficient interest to make them want to discuss it.

When I was actually in the car on the way to the school, one of the ladies in charge of my appearance began to explain to me that they uh hadn't uh exactly been able to follow out my wishes and uh they hoped I wouldn't be too upset. Their original plan had been for me to speak to the gifted-and-talented program, which was made up of about fifty seventh, eighth, and ninth graders. (I gasped.) But they'd gotten fouled up. It seems that the special reading teacher had read *The Great Gilly Hopkins* out loud to her class, and when she heard that I was going to be at the school, had simply demanded that her class be allowed to horn in on the gifted-and-talented's special event. So there I was with about seventy junior high students to enthrall. Much to my surprise, not to say relief, the session went all right. I wasn't sure who was from the gifted program and who was from the special reading class, the questions were more or less of the ordinary variety. But I did notice a boy in a red sweat shirt sitting several feet away from everyone else in the room who was giving me more than ordinary attention. After the program was over, he came up and hung around until the other students had left, and then he began to ask me about Gilly. Who was she? Where was she? Then he wanted to know all the other stories— the things that had happened that somehow hadn't gotten into the book. It was one of those times when you know the real question is not being voiced, but I didn't understand what it was. Finally, a teacher persuaded the boy that he must return to class, and besides, she explained, I had to catch a plane shortly. When he had gone, the librarian told me that Eddie was a member of the special reading class who had heard *Gilly* read. Like Gilly, he was battling his way through a world of trouble. He had never shown any particular positive interest in books or school until his teacher had read *Gilly* to the class. And suddenly he had a passion. He was wild about a book—one of those reluctant readers, or even nonreaders, who had to this point seen words, not to mention books, as the deadliest of enemies.

I thought about Eddie for days. Here was a real-live Gilly who not only approved of but actually liked my fictional one. It was better than having a Japanese like *The Master Puppeteer*. Well, I decided, I'll just send him a copy. Even if he won't ever read it. At least he will own a book he likes. And that will be one for our side, now won't it?

Just before *Gilly* won the National Book Award, I got a letter from Eddie, and as some of you may remember, I read his letter with, I hasten to assure you, his permission, as part of my acceptance speech. But it feels so good to hear it that I'm going to repeat it.

Dear Mrs. Paterson,
Thank you for the book "The Great Gilly Hopkins." I love the book. I am on page 16.

Your friend
Always
Eddie Young

And Eddie didn't stop on page 16. He's read the book four times. He's also read *Bridge to Terabithia,* and in his last letter he said he was starting on *The Master Puppeteer.* I rushed off a "Now don't be discouraged by all those long Japanese names" letter to him. I don't know as I write this if he finished it, or even if he's read any other books since he learned that books are not fearsome enemies. I hope he has. I believe he will.

But somebody, you see, had to make the connection for him. Someone had to first give him the words. His teacher did it by reading to him what he would not have, perhaps at the time could not have, read for himself. Then she fought against the administration and the rules of a fussy writer to get Eddie in to hear me speak. She believed that Eddie had a right to the words—that he had a need for the words, even if no one else, not even Eddie, believed that he did.

I love to tell this story because it was my words that Eddie's teacher used. More often it will not be my book but someone else's that works this magic for a child. Indeed, when I told the story of Eddie to my friend, the reading teacher, her face brightened and she told me the story of her own son, who shunned books, even though his mother was a teacher of reading and his father a librarian. Suddenly at nine, not to be outdone by a younger sister, he had picked up a children's classic version of Robin Hood, determined to get through one book cover to cover to prove to his seven-year-old sister that he wasn't as dumb as she thought he was. He read all day and into the night and came to his mother the next morning with tears streaming down his cheeks. It was the best book, he declared, that he had *ever* read. It didn't seem to occur to him that it was the *only* book he had ever read. Of course, it was just the first. But it was there when he needed it.

In all the furor about the right to read and basic education, there is often, it seems to me, something missing. Why are we so determined to teach our children to read? So that they can read road signs? Of course. Make out a job application? Of course. Figure out the destination of the bus so that they can get to work? Yes, of course. But don't we want far more for them than the ability to decode? Don't we want for them the life and growth and refreshment that only the full richness of our language can give? And when I say this I am saying with Joan Didion that we fail our children if all we give them are the platitudes, the clichés, the slogans of our society, which we throw out whole to keep from having to think or feel deeply.

We cannot give them what we do not have. We cannot share what we do not care for deeply ourselves. If we prescribe books as medicine, our children have a perfect right to refuse the nasty-tasting spoon.

I was always told that I should read the *Odyssey*. It popped up in small doses in English and Latin textbooks as I was growing up. But somehow I never got around to the whole thing until I was forty-six years old. My daughter Mary and I were going on a trip to Greece, and I gave myself the assignment to read the *Odyssey* all the way through from beginning to end. Do you know why the *Odyssey* has lasted for nearly three thousand years? Because it is a simply marvelous story. Why did people keep telling me that I *ought* to read it so I could be an educated person? Was it because they had never read it themselves but had always meant to? I can't imagine anyone who had ever read it, certainly not in Rouse's translation, anyone who had ever really read it, telling someone else to read it because it was good for him. Read it because it's one of the best stories you'll ever read. Read it because it's one of the best stories I ever read.

17

And when you close Homer, there are the books of Jane Austen and Joseph Conrad, and great fat volumes of Tolstoy. There is the *Bible,* perhaps the most overprescribed and least taken of any. There is Flannery O'Connor and Anne Tyler. There is William Shakespeare and Jacob Bronowski. There is *The Yearling* and *A Tale of Two Cities.* There is *The Secret Garden* and *The Wind in the Willows.* There is *Ramona the Brave* and *Where the Wild Things Are.* I have only begun to name what I especially love. There are countless others—really good books. Good or even great because they make the right connections. They pull together for us a world that is falling apart. They are the words that integrate us, stretch us, judge us, comfort and heal us. They are the words that mirror the Word of creation, bringing order out of chaos.

I believe we must try, always conscious of our own fragmentary knowledge and nature, to give our children these words. I know as you do that words can be used for evil as well as good. But we must take that risk. We must try as best we are able to give our children words that will shape their minds so they can make those miraculous leaps of imagination that no sinless computer will ever be able to rival—those connections in science, in art, in the living of this life that will reveal the little truths. For it is these little truths that point to the awesome, unknowable unity, the Truth, which holds us together and makes us members one of another.

VELMA VARNER LECTURE
(December 8, 1979)

18

DOG DAY WONDER

❦

It was the sort of hot and humid day in late August that I just hoped to get through without snapping off the children's heads at the neckline—not the sort, surely, upon which I expected to receive a wonderful gift from one of the very children I was threatening to decapitate. At about noon David brought me a cicada, which he had earlier discovered coming out of the ground. "I think it's about ready to shed its skin," he said. "Watch."

You would think that a dog day cicada would sense that it had a bare two days to live and get on with emerging, but it took its own sweet time. First a tiny slit in the back, then, very gradually, it was as though it had pulled down a waist-length zipper. A hint of color began to show in the narrow slit. The extremities grew brown as limbs were eased out of the old armor. The eyes dulled as the living ones were withdrawn. And then the colors: I never would have believed them—a pure Caribbean green, yellow, aqua, cream, beige, and flecks of gold like jewelry on the head.

When almost out, its wings bits of crumpled ribbon at its sides, our cicada still clung to the old brown shell, which now seemed half again too small for its splendid body. By this time we had watched for nearly an hour, but we weren't impatient. All our life processes had slowed down, so captivated were we by its metamorphosis. At long last the wings stretched out, transparent except for hairline veins of green and yellow.

Suddenly, in the only swift move we saw, it swung like a circus acrobat from the dry sarcophagus to the twig from which the discarded shell still hung. We swelled with pride. Our cicada had made it.

We left it then, checking from time to time. The glorious colors of the newly emergent cicada darkened in time to a rich black, though its belly remained a lighter shade, and it still wore gold upon its head. At about four o'clock the twig was empty. Our cicada had flown to the oak tree to breed and die, oblivious to the wake of wonder it had left behind.

As I let that wonder wash over me I realized that this was the gift I really wanted to give my children, for what good are straight teeth and trumpet lessons to a person who cannot see the grandeur that the world is charged with? In her book, *The Sense of Wonder*, Rachel Carson says that if she had influence over the good fairy who gives gifts to children at their christening, she would ask the fairy to give each child "a sense of wonder so indestructible that it would last throughout life, as an unfailing antidote against the boredom and disenchantment of later years, the sterile occupation with things that are artificial, the alienation from the sources of our strength."[1]

Pity we can't tap that fairy resource. Or is it? Isn't wonder a truly human characteristic? In fact, I don't even subscribe to that well-worn platitude that children are born with a sense of wonder that becomes dulled in the pursuit of living. Children are born with a wholesome sense of curiosity, I won't argue that, but wonder is more than curiosity. It demands an element of awe, a marveling that takes time and wisdom to supply. Both Rachel Carson and her nephew Roger, for whom she wrote her book, had a sense of wonder, but I defy anyone to prove that his sense, simply because he was a child, was of a higher quality than hers. As the book shows, Roger caught his sense of wonder from his aunt, who never tried to teach him natural history. She simply shared with him something that had filled her with wonder, saying: "Watch" or "Listen" or "Smell."

Thus, to follow Miss Carson's lead, if I want my children to develop an indestructible sense of wonder, then I must first develop my own. There have been times—that twilight when we saw the double rainbow spanning Lake George and snatched all the children out of bed to run to the lakeside and watch until it faded into the dusk—or when the riot of summer stars drove us right out of our car into an open field to bend our necks back and gape and gaze. But as I joyfully recall these rare moments, I am sobered to realize how often I must be missing other chances for wonder, which like dog day cicada, are all about me humming in the trees.

[1]Rachel Carson, *The Sense of Wonder* (New York: Harper & Row, 1965), pp. 42–43.

'Tis ye, 'tis your estranged faces,
That miss the many-splendored thing.

What I desire, then, for myself and for my children is a face not estranged but expectant—a sense of wonder on the way to becoming both indestructible and contagious.

From PARENTS' CHOICE
(January/February 1979)

READING AND WRITING

Benjamin Disraeli said that "the author who speaks about his own books is almost as bad as a mother who talks about her own children." The fact that I must plead guilty on both counts in no way mitigates the indictment. There are real problems when a writer talks about her own books. You can't talk about them while you're writing them, at least I can't. They're too fragile and would collapse under the weight of your verbiage. Once they're safely written, but not yet published might be a good time, but you may be the only person interested in the book at that point. And even if you aren't, it would be grossly unfair, because no one else would be in a position to talk back. After the book is published, you're already hard at work on another book and can't remember what you said in the previous book or exactly why, so when people ask you questions about it, you begin to develop a kind of mythology about the book. It becomes almost impossible to recall why you said a certain thing the way you did, but as you reflect upon it, you come up with some rather interesting answers, which may or may not be factual. Your critical faculties also begin to come into play. You read a passage and not only forget why you wrote it but can hardly believe you would have or that your peerless editor could have let you get away with it.

The best people to talk about a book, then, are not writers, but readers. I am no Benjamin Disraeli, but I do have my little philosophies. My philosophy of publication goes something like this: Once a book is published, it no longer belongs to me. My creative task is done. The work now belongs to the creative mind of my readers. I had my turn to make of it what I would, now it is their turn. I have no more right to tell readers how they should respond to what I have written than they had to tell me how to write it. It's a wonderful feeling when readers hear what I thought I was trying to say, but there is no law that they must. Frankly, it is even more thrilling for a reader to find something in my writing that I hadn't until that moment known was there. But this happens because of who the reader is, not simply because of who I am or what I have done.

Recently I was talking with a former college professor of mine, the man, I suppose more than any other, who taught me how to write. We were talking not about any of my books but about Ursala LeGuin's *The Tombs of Atuan,* which I urged him to read. He began to speak about the powerful range of emotion that the book had evoked in him and wondered aloud if it was really suitable for children. "How could a young reader bear it?" he asked me. "I could hardly bear it myself." What I said to him rather inarticulately is the point I'm still fumbling to make. It was that what he had experienced in reading that book was not simply what the genius of the writer had put there (and I do not underestimate the genius), but the whole emotional history of a beautiful sixty-year-old life responding to that story. His creative genius had made a powerful book even more powerful. Dr. Winship is by nature and by discipline a great reader, just as Mrs. LeGuin is by nature and by discipline a great writer.

The fact that Dr. Winship is a great reader does not mean that everything he touches turns to gold. He once told a class of dropping a book called *World Enough and Time* after a chapter and a half, concluding that he had neither. So there must be something in the book itself to evoke a powerful response from a reader. It's not hard to recognize that something when a book has it, but to describe what it is or duplicate the effect—ah, there's the rub.

One Sunday night we were watching the episode in the PBS life of Dickens that contained the reaction of the reading public to the death of Little Nell. It was marvelously done, piling scene upon scene of persons all over England weeping unashamedly over what sounded suspiciously to me, my husband, and my eleven-year-old, as a clear case of criminal overwriting. I hasten to say we were hearing it entirely out of context, but we were screaming with laughter at the distress of Dickens's readers. How could anyone, much less the entire English-speaking world, have fallen to pieces over the death of a child in a magazine serial? Maybe it was funny because I've never read *The Old Curiosity Shop*. I do remember quite clearly reading through the whole of *Tale of Two Cities* perfectly dry-eyed, closing the book, going to my bed, and crying inconsolably for a long, long time.

Of course, I've been tricked into crying on more than one occasion by what I can recognize perfectly well as cheap sentimentality, so I don't put any ultimate value on my own tears, taken by themselves. But there are books, some of them by Dickens, that have drawn from me a depth of response that makes me know that this book—no, not this book, these persons (or in several notable cases, these animals) are no longer figments of an author's imagination—these persons are alive in me, part of my life from that time on.

How does a writer do this? I don't know. I really don't know. I'm not trying to be coy. I certainly can't speak for Ursula LeGuin or Charles Dickens. But as the only writer I know well enough to talk about, I feel a need to try to describe a process I don't understand. It's something like a seed that grows in the dark, and one day you look and there is a full-grown plant with a flower on it—or a grain of sand that keeps rubbing at your vitals until you find you are building a coating around it. I think that's why it takes me a long time to write a book. The physical act of setting it down on a page doesn't take so long, but the growth of a book takes time, and most of it happens out of sight like a kind of dream work. And why it should happen inside me instead of inside someone else, I have no idea. It makes no more sense to me that I should be a writer than that I should have curly hair. I am conscious of feeding the process, though even this is indirect. I read, I think, I talk, I look, I listen, I hate, I fear, I love, I weep, and somehow all of my life gets wrapped around the grain. I don't get a perfect pearl every time, but then, neither does the oyster. (The trick is to know which ones to string and which ones to cast away.)

What I'm trying to say is that to me writing and reading are both gifts, neither of which has meaning without the other.

Now the gift of creative reading, like all natural gifts, must be nourished or it will atrophy. And you nourish it, in much the same way you nourish the gift of writing—you read, think, talk, look, listen, hate, fear, love, weep—and bring all of your life like a sieve to what you read. That which is not worthy of your gift will quickly pass through, but the gold remains. I can feel this metaphor crumbling about my ears, because a sieve is a passive thing and creative reading is not. It can take a modest pearl and set it off by its own experience in such a way that it will give off a luster never imagined by the oyster/writer working away between his shells in the darkness. And the reader will say humbly to the writer: What a beautiful pearl you made! And I hope the writer will be honest enough to know that she has been twice blessed—once with the gift of the pearl and again with the gift of a reader who could receive and cherish what was, after all, simply a natural response to a pain in the stomach.

THE CASE OF THE CURIOUS BABY-SITTER

LEAVE WELL ENOUGH ALONE
by Rosemary Wells

"Oh what a tangled web we weave,
When first we practice to deceive!"

<small>(As quoted by Sister Elizabeth MacIntosh,
by Dorothy Coughlin, Freshman,
Sacred Heart Academy, Newburgh,
and recalled—with appropriate guilt—
New York, 1956.)
Sir Walter Scott</small>

Dorothy Coughlin is an Irish Catholic policeman's daughter who spends the summer after her first year in high school as a mother's helper on a wealthy estate outside Philadelphia. Dorothy's upbringing (one in which salvation is not so much by either faith or works as by platitude) has ill prepared her for the pleasures and pitfalls of life among the Hoades.

The household consists of the two spoiled, but anxious little charges, a handsome, but curiously crude Mr. Hoade, and his wife, a scatterbrained near alcoholic. It is Mrs. Hoade's total lack of Sacred Heart Academy's vaunted virtues of discipline, organization, and concentration that serves to warn Dorothy of what, unreformed, she herself might well become and to stir her sympathies.

There are two more members of the family, unseen, but all the more disturbing in their absence—a mongoloid baby, who, Mrs. Hoade has told her daughters, has a "bad cold," and thus must live in isolation in the cottage across the field with her German nurse—and a great-grandmother who, the mother explains, has gone to a kind of resort for "elderly people who want to have a little vacation."

But Maria Hoade is a liar. Dorothy, who was caught lying to Reverend Mother in front of the school assembly, understands why a person might lie, but still she just can't seem to leave Mrs. Hoade's lies alone.

I began this book laughing with delight at Rosemary Wells's marvelous re-creation of fourteenness—the fervid rejoicing over a mistake not made, the strain of drinking a Coke noiselessly in the presence of an adult one is struggling to impress, furtively removing and disposing of one's ruined stockings, only to have them returned by a smiling porter. And for those of us who grew up pious in the forties and fifties, there is that ever-losing battle for goodness—the feverish yielding to the very temptation one has seconds before praised God for the power to overcome.

I began the book laughing. I ended it in goose bumps. In between I had gobbled up red herrings like gumdrops.

To say that Wells deceived me right up until the next-to-the-last page is to acknowledge her ability as a writer of suspense, but it is the shimmering threads of humor and human insight with which she has spun her tale that completely entrap the reader.

From THE WASHINGTON POST BOOK WORLD
(May 1, 1977)

CREATIVITY LIMITED

Novels for Young People Today

⋙§෴

I had been writing fiction for years with hardly anyone noticing, when, suddenly, a book of mine won a National Book Award and overnight I seemed to have opinions worth consulting. "Dear Mrs. Paterson," one correspondent asked, "do you think civilization as we know it will survive the twentieth century?" "Dear Mr. So-and-so," I replied, "I don't know at four o'clock what I'll be having for supper at six, a matter which is almost entirely under my control."

Most questions were less cosmic and more relevant, like the one asked me by an editor friend at the end of a business call. "Oh, by the way," she said, "while I've got you on the phone, what is your theory of creativity?" She wanted a quotation for an article she was writing. What she got was several minutes of stammering at the prime daytime rate.

In order not to be caught like that again, I began to read articles and books about creativity. Incidentally, the word "creativity" doesn't even appear in my *Oxford English Dictionary*, 1971 edition. Aside from the fact that the word didn't exist until quite recently, the chief thing I learned about creativity is that students of human behavior seem to know very little about what it is. Psychiatrists writing about it were either reduced to poetry or else they sought to explain it as some kind of neurosis. The one point that seemed to make sense to me out of my research was a point Rollo May makes in *The Courage to Create*. That is—there is no such thing as unlimited creativity. It is within limits, often very narrow limits, that a creative work comes into being.

I am as concerned about freedom as the next American, but freedom is quite different from the lack of limitations. Let me illustrate. Very often people ask me, "How do you find time to write?" The first time I remember being asked this question it was by a woman who worked a forty-hour week outside her home. I was puzzled. "How do *you* find time to work?" I asked, feeling her life was far more complex than mine. But she didn't see it as the same thing at all. Instead she began to list what she saw as my limitations. You have four lively children. Your husband is a church pastor. You have three PTA's, choir, church activities, et cetera, et cetera. At last I realized that the questioner was assuming that my husband's work and my children's activities were limitations that enslaved me, whereas I felt that they were the very boundaries that gave form to my life.

You'll remember that Boris Pasternak had a great dread of being deported. He felt that, if he were forced out of Russia, he would no longer be able to write. Russia was for him a necessary limitation. "Don't you wish," I am asked, "don't you wish you could just sail away alone to a Caribbean Isle and write all day?" Never. "What? No, never?" Well, hardly ever. The more perceptive question came from a critic who knows my work almost better than I do. "Your writing is so bound up with your children," she said. "What are you going to do when they all grow up?" For a moment I had a hint of the panic Pasternak must have felt when threatened with deportation. But only for a moment. I've lived long enough to know that in this world there is rarely a shortage on limitations. There'll be plenty more when I need them.

Now life is often a parable for art. Many of the same people who worry that I don't have time to write are bothered by my choice of form. "Don't you feel constricted writing for children?" they'll ask. William, don't you find fourteen tightly rhymed lines an absolute prison? Ah, Pablo, if you could just yank that picture off that lousy scrap of canvas! You get the point. Form is not a bar to free expression, but the boundaries within which writers and artists freely choose to work.

You choose an art form, says C. S. Lewis, in one of his most quoted sentences, because it is the best form for something you have to say. It seems to me, therefore, more than a little silly to complain that your freedom has been restricted by the form you chose.

The library promotion staff at Crowell Junior Books say that I write novels for ages ten and up. When I examine books intended for this audience, my first observation is how few special limitations there seem to be.

There is, for example, no apparent limitation on vocabulary or sentence structure. A writer for *The Washingtonian Magazine* did a reading-level test on my book *The Master Puppeteer*. He reported to his readers that it fell comfortably between the seventh- and eighth-grade levels, which is just where the publisher claims it belongs. But the writer went on to say that he had applied the same test to Erica Jong's *Fear of Flying. Flying*, he said, had come out at the sixth-grade level. These are matters beyond my knowledge, but I do know that I spend an inordinate amount of time with my nose in dictionaries trying to develop a vocabulary worthy of my readers.

Okay, okay, you can use big words if you want to. You'll have to admit, the protester cries from the back row, that your subject matter is restricted. I can only speak from experience. My editor has never tried to restrict me. Let me offer a brief and brutal survey of my already published novels for children and young adults. In the first, the hero is a bastard, and the chief female character ends up in a brothel. In the second, the heroine has an illicit love affair, her mother dies in a plague, and most of her companions commit suicide. In the third, which is full of riots in the streets, the hero's best friend is permanently maimed. In the fourth, a central child character dies in an accident. In the fifth, turning away from the mayhem in the first four, I wrote what I refer to as my "funny book." In it the heroine merely fights, lies, steals, cusses, bullies an emotionally disturbed child, and acts out her racial bigotry in a particularly vicious manner.

You may not be surprised to know that I do from time to time receive letters of protest from teachers and librarians. You may be amazed to know that the only element in any of my books that any of these adults has complained to me about is the occasional profanity. Characters in young people's novels should be permitted to do anything, it would seem, except cuss. I can only perceive this as a testimony to the power of words.

But back to subject matter. When I examine a bald recitation of the events depicted in my books, I come away slightly shocked. What could I have been thinking of? Yet, somehow, when a story is coming to life, I'm not judging it as appropriate or inappropriate, I'm living through it. In *The Sign of the Chrysanthe-mum* Akiko ended up in a brothel not because I wanted to scandalize my readers, not because I'm advocating legal prostitution, but because in twelfth-century Japan, a beautiful thirteen-year-old-girl with no protector would have ended up in a brothel. And the penniless boy who loved her would indeed have been powerless to save her. I didn't want to make Akiko a prostitute, but there was no way out. It did occur to me afterward that I hadn't seen a lot of books for young readers along this line, but twelve years ago, when I was writing this story, I was being torn apart that such a thing did and does happen to children in this world. If we compare subject matter as my friend at *The Washingtonian Magazine* compared reading levels, I note that the adult best seller at the time my book was being readied for market—the adult best seller that was breaking every sales record since *Gone With the Wind*—was the story of an overachieving sea gull.

If the limitations inherent to my form are not in reading level or subject matter, where are they? I am going to tell you where the boundaries are for me, realizing that you will be able to cite a gate for every fence.

First, a book for young readers has to tell a story. This may seem self-evident, but the truth is some people ignore it because plotting is very hard work. When I'm hearing myself introduced as a "great natural storyteller," it is all I can do to keep from leaping to my feet to object. Great natural storytellers don't spend countless days hewing a story line out of rock with a straight pin, now do they? Yet it's got to be done. I received an anguished letter from a yet unpublished writer, in which she asked, "Isn't there any place for the plotless teenage novel?" I could only think of one. As burdensome as the limitation of plot may seem to be, it is not one I'm willing to circumvent. I simply don't like novels that aren't going anywhere, and I can't imagine many readers who do.

A second limitation on the novel for the young is length. Now there are plenty of exceptions to this one. *Watership Down* and *The Lord of the Rings* were written by the authors as stories for their own children. But these days a novel for the young usually runs under two hundred pages. Unlike plotting, this perfectly suits my natural tendencies. I am one of those people who write short. A great deal of my revision time is spent fleshing out and very little in cutting. When I first began to think seriously about writing, I assumed that this quality of mine would lead me into the world of the short story. So I wrote short story upon short story, selling practically nothing. I think the truth of the matter is that I am not basically a short-story writer. I am a novelist who writes short novels.

This is closely related to what I see as a third limitation. Intricacy, density, design—I'm not sure what to call it, but when I read Mary Lee Settle's *Blood Tie*, Anne Tyler's *Celestial Navigation*, or John Fowles's *Daniel Martin*, I hear a symphony orchestra. When I read my own *Bridge to Terabithia*, I hear a flute solo, unaccompanied. Occasionally, to be sure, you get a decent adult novel along the flute-solo line, but most truly fine adult novels are extremely complex works of art. Some eleven-year-olds are reading Dickens and Austen, but most are not. And I, even when I'm dealing with an almost impossibly complicated situation like the Gempei War in twelfth-century Japan, tend to hear through all the storm and clamor a rather simple melody.

A writer is also limited, you see, by who she is. As Flannery O'Connor wrote to a young writer friend: "There is only one answer . . . and that is that one writes what one can. Vocation implies limitation but few people realize it who don't actually practice an art."[1] So when people ask me why I write what I do, I take comfort from one of my heroines. Flannery O'Connor wrote what she could; I write what I can.

A fourth limitation has to do with characters. They may be any age, and, indeed, any species, but they must be characters a reader can care about. This is another of those limitations I can rejoice in. When I am reading a novel and discover that the author has contempt for the people he has created, I am furious. If he despises these who are flesh of his flesh, what right does he have to inflict them on me? I don't want to waste my energy reading, and certainly not my energy writing about people I hate. Even if I start a book with a satisfying villain, I seem doomed to care for that person before the end.

There is certainly room in the world of books for entertainment, but for the serious writer of fiction for the young there is a fifth limitation, that of theme, for she will want to write not only a story that is going somewhere but a story about something that matters deeply. I would like to share with you the best explanation of the importance of theme in books for young people that I have ever heard. It comes from Jill Paton Walsh's 1978 Whitthall Lecture at the Library of Congress.

"When I was young," she says, "my grandfather tried to teach me to play chess, which he deeply loved and wanted to share with me. And he got me horribly confused. Like most good players, he was not really interested in opening games. No sooner did I get far enough to advance a king's pawn timidly

[1]Flannery O'Connor, *The Habit of Being: Letters* (New York: Farrar, Straus & Giroux, 1979), p. 221.

two paces than he was telling me about six thousand possibilities in the middle game opened up by such a beginning, and six thousand others by the same act excluded; and the more he spoke the less I understood him.

"How often," she continues, "I recollect that situation when I read adult novels. They are treatises on the complexities of the middle game, written by and for players of some skill. My grandfather was not wrong to point out to me the consequences of an opening game, which does indeed condition the middle game; but he had forgotten to tell me about checkmate, and you cannot play at all unless you know how the game is won and lost, and what will count as an ending. That is why it is necessary in children's books to mirror death, to show a projected end, to teach that nothing is forever, so that the child may know the nature of the game he is playing and may take a direction, make purposeful moves. It is the plain truth that human life is passing, and that we must find what we will value in the world, and how we will live in the light of that." [2]

That is why, you see, I do find the strong themes of my books appropriate for young readers. Like Jill Paton Walsh, I want them to see the nature of the game we are all engaged in so that they may make purposeful moves.

And in the shadow of this rather grand limitation, I find a more personal one. I will not take a young reader through a story and in the end abandon him. That is, I will not write a book that closes in despair. I cannot, will not, withhold from my young readers the harsh realities of human hunger and suffering and loss, but neither will I neglect to plant that stubborn seed of

[2]Jill Paton Walsh, "The Lords of Time," Whittall Lecture, Library of Congress, Nov. 13, 1978. Published in the *Library of Congress Quarterly* (Spring 1979).

hope that has enabled our race to outlast wars and famines and the destruction of death.

If you think that this is the limitation that will keep me forever a writer for the young, perhaps it is. I don't mind. I do what I can and do it joyfully.

From THE WRITER
(December 1980)

RAMONA REDUX

⚒᠊ᢌ

RAMONA AND HER FATHER
by Beverly Cleary
ILLUSTRATED BY ALAN TIEGREEN

Her many friends will rejoice to know that on the precarious journey toward growing up, Ramona Q has somehow slipped through the double binds of Mrs. Griggs's first grade into grade two, her gutsy soul intact. She can read now without mentally buzzing all the unknown words, and, while her spelling may leave something to be desired, it's quite sufficient for signs like:

NOSMO

KING

which are vital in her campaign to save her father's life.

Ramona Quimby, once known as Ramona the Pest, is the kind of child that drives her elders to the brink. If they could only understand that the hair full of burs, which must be cut out one by one, started out as a magnificent crown, rather like the one that magically appears on the head of the boy in the margarine commercial. Ramona had placed the crown of burs on her head while practicing earnestly for a career in television advertising. She needs to make a million dollars to save her family, especially her father, who has lost his job and is starting to get crabby and smoke too much. Ramona, like many of her tribe, never, or hardly ever, sets out to be malicious, and she's certainly not thoughtless. Her schemes are painstakingly crafted and bravely launched, only to be dashed again and again on the uncharted rocks of the grown-up world.

Beverly Cleary, Ramona's creator and winner of the Laura Ingalls Wilder Award for her contribution to children's literature, has written more than twenty books for young readers over at least that many years. She is, and I do not exaggerate, wildly popular with children. So I came to her books, not only as a reviewer but as a writer, to ask why.

Is it because she is easy to read? She is, but so is "Run, Spot, Run." Is it because her settings are contemporary and her characters familiar? They are, but there are thousands of books fitting both descriptions that never capture a fraction of Cleary's devoted readership.

Last week I carried home a stack of Cleary books from the local library to see if I could discover her secret. My two teenagers spotted the books on the dining room table and smiles spread across their faces. "Oh, yeah," one said, as though hearing the name of an old friend after many years. "I remember reading those." "Yeah," said the other. "They're funny."

When I was young there were two kinds of funny—funny ha-ha and funny peculiar. A lot of funny ha-ha things happen in Cleary's books, but her real specialty is another kind of funny, which is a cross between funny ha-ha and funny ahhh. Cleary has the rare gift of being able to reveal us to ourselves while still keeping an arm around our shoulder. We laugh (ha ha) to recognize that funny, peculiar little self we were and are and then laugh (ahhh) with relief that we've been understood at last.

The librarian from whom I borrowed the books said that Cleary is loved because she can describe simply the complex feelings of a child. But even more, Cleary is able to sketch clearly with a few perfect strokes the inexplicable adult world as seen through a child's eyes. *Ramona the Brave* should be required reading for all teachers, just as *Ramona and Her Father* should be read by all parents, though Ramona's parents are, in my grandmother's phrase, "far above the average." (I take the liberty of quoting my grandmother because Mr. Quimby, of whom I am particularly fond, is always quoting his.)

Amidst the traps and hurdles strewn along the path toward growing up (people are always telling Ramona to "grow up!" and she's trying, really she is!), there are rare patches of undiluted joy. Cleary captures these as gently as my eleven-year-old catches fireflies. Who will ever forget the day Ramona and her friend Howie make tin-can stilts and clank clank through the twilight, singing "Ninety-nine bottles of beer on the wall" all the way down to the last bottle? Or the Christmas pageant for which Ramona's harassed mother has only had time to devise a sheep costume out of faded pajamas, upon which prance, sometimes upside down, an army of pink bunnies? Howie's grandmother has made him and his bratty baby sister, who doesn't even need one, glorious sheepskins of woolly acrylic with zippers up the front. I won't tell you how this particular mortification is transformed into joy. Read it aloud with someone you love. I've asked my nine-year-old to read it to me. She loves Cleary, too, and is less likely than I to spill tears all over page 186.

From THE WASHINGTON POST BOOK WORLD
(October 9, 1977)

A SONG OF INNOCENCE
AND EXPERIENCE

◆◇◆

In a brochure for a summer institute at the Center for the Study of Children's Literature at Simmons College, at which one of my books was to be studied, there was a question from F. R. Leavis that the participants were to ask of each of the books they read. "How significant are the works not only in terms of form and structure but 'in terms of the human awareness they promote, awareness of the possibilities of life?'"

Now I come from the theological tradition, in which it is heresy to take a verse out of context, so I dutifully went to the Old Dominion University library and looked up *The Great Tradition* by Leavis, in order to examine the setting for this test of value that he is advancing. I found to my distress that Leavis is using it as a means of separating the artistic sheep from the entertaining goats—the (in his words) "few really great—the major novelists" from such minor literary lights as Anthony

Trollope, Henry Fielding, and Charles Dickens. These, according to Leavis, are entertainers, not artists.

The first defense that occurred is the defense of modesty. I could say to that that art is Tolstoy and Austen and Conrad, and that I have never presumed to those heights. That, if Charles Dickens is an entertainer, so am I. That way I couldn't flunk the exam. I never enrolled in the course. The grade meant nothing. It is a line of argument that has rather obvious appeal. The problem with it is that I never set out to be an entertainer, so if there is to be a division into two classes, I cannot in any conscience escape the test on the grounds that entertainment was my goal.

Caroline Gordon, in her book *How to Read a Novel*, gives an example that makes very clear for me the distinction between art and entertainment.

> . . . the man who has spent the evening reading Sherlock Holmes in an easy chair, before a blazing fire, is not likely to act differently toward his fellow creatures the next morning, no matter how much he admires Sir Arthur Conan Doyle's masterly creation. On the other hand, the man who succeeds in finishing the reading of *War and Peace*—not everybody does—may not feel himself the same man afterward, and this change of heart may reflect itself so clearly in his daily conduct that other people will recognize the change.[1]

Art, according to this definition, has the power to change life. To read a great novel is to lay yourself open for a conversion experience. Another distinction I might make as an aside is that you don't speed-read art. When I see or hear those boasts of a

---

[1]Caroline Gordon, *How to Read a Novel* (New York: The Viking Press, 1957), p. 12.

speed-reading-school graduate having read *Jaws* in an hour, I am pleased—think of all the time he's saved. But when someone brags to me that he's read *War and Peace* in five hours, I get sick to my stomach. You do not read *War and Peace* in five hours or even five days. You live for a season with Natasha and Pierre and André, and when at last you come to young Nicholas Bolkonski's words: ". . . Oh, Father, Father! Yes, I will do something with which even *he* would be satisfied. . . ." you are simply not the same person who weeks before opened the book and read: "Well, Prince, so Genoa and Lucca are now just family estates of the Buonapartes." You might be hard put to describe in mere words exactly what transformation has taken place between the reading of those two sentences, but you know that you will never be the same.

And isn't it significant that you have trouble putting that experience into words? Isn't it because the truly great novelists have not changed you by their power to manipulate your intellect so much as they have captured your senses and borne away your emotions? And the true artist is never a manipulator anyway. Although this change has taken place in you beneath the level of rational explanations, it has taken place, not against your will, but with your eager, even joyful, collaboration.

The longer I think about the conversion experience that is at the core of art, the more terrified I become. Because I know that, however I may fail, this is what my intent has been and must continue to be. With every book I have written there is a reader whose life I have been determined to change.

There are all kinds of things wrong with the statement I just made, and if you are not scandalized by it, you certainly ought to be. From the viewpoint of psychology it is appalling and from the standards of theology it is heresy. No human being has the right, even if she had the power, to change another human being.

Let me step back for a minute and talk about the person I am writing for. I am, like many of you, a reader of *The Horn Book Magazine*. I read all the reviews, of course, to get my own grade as well as to gauge my class standing, but I also read the articles. The problem with the articles is that I have trouble ridding myself of a state of general awe when I read them. I assume almost without question that the writer, whoever he or she might be, is far more of an expert than I, and I would do well to shut up and pay attention. Actually, this is usually a pretty safe course of action, but every now and then as I am respectfully reading along, a writer will say something that so jars me, that I am forced to stop nodding and bowing and take some time to glue myself back together.

For just over a year now I have been rearranging myself after the encounter with Aidan Chambers's article entitled "Three Fallacies about Children's Books." Speaking of flunking, I discovered that I was to a greater or lesser extent a supporter of all three fallacies. I won't take time to discuss strikes one and two, but strike three was the one that hurt the most, and is the one relevant to what I am saying. It is, according to Mr. Chambers, a fallacy to reply, when asked why one writes for children, "I do not write for children, I write for myself."[2]

In a very real sense, I do write for myself. The parallel that comes to mind most readily is those many times when as a child I played by myself. During that time I invented elaborate fantasies and played them out, taking all the roles, often

[2]Aidan Chambers, "Three Fallacies about Children's Books," *The Horn Book* (June 1978).

speaking aloud for each role in turn. Now these games were truly for myself alone. The last thing that I wanted was an audience. I would have been mortified by an audience. It is the same when I am in the first draft of a book. During this period, I am totally absorbed in the story for its own sake. I am embarrassed if anyone sees the draft ahead of time. I won't even tell my husband what I am about. At that stage I really believe, fallacy or not, that what I am doing is for myself.

And yet, as Jill Paton Walsh pointed out to me when we were discussing this question, there is an audience from the very beginning—a reader whose presence I often forget all about, but who is always there. This reader is myself as a child.

So when a minute ago, I said that in every book, there is a reader I am determined to change, I am now forced to confess that that reader is myself. But that only makes my statement slightly less scandalous. Why, if I am writing to convert myself, am I inflicting the process on thousands of innocent children who are in no way responsible for my deficiencies as a human being?

The answer to this question, which is no answer at all, is that I am a novelist. A novel, as Caroline Gordon points out, is different from other forms of art in that it "concerns itself with the conduct of life. . . . life as it manifests itself in change, in action." And in this I am limited, as every novelist is limited, because I have only one life, one entrance into the sum of human experience. And though it is the height of arrogance to believe that this one life of mine is of any interest, not to mention any help, to other lives, it is the only life I have to offer.

But why children? If I am, in fact, writing to change myself, a forty-six-year-old woman, why don't I have the decency to publish for other forty-six-year-old women and leave the innocent children out of it? If you are a conscientious writer of books for children, all you need to do to guarantee a gray head overnight is to read the standards set by one of your gifted colleagues. The article entitled "Who Should Write for Young Readers?" was written by Maia Wojciechowska and said in part:

> First of all you must be a natural *admirer* of children. You must be one of those people who instinctively knows that children are the truly *beautiful* people. You must be aware of the magnificent beginning that is the lot of every human being, a beginning that is invariably loused up by people who don't recognize children as a superior breed. Children are more intelligent than adults. The directness of their thought processes must be the delight of logicians. They can write any adult under the table as readily as they can put to shame any painter.[3]

I live in a house with four of this superior breed who are, in my grandmother's words, "far above the average." But as beautiful as they are, believe me, their father and I greet with shouts of joy every millimeter on the road to maturity. And I confess, if I must believe that they are doomed to go only backward from this point, I'm not sure I want to stay around for the trip.

I brag about their intelligence and abilities, but no one can convince me that there is one among them who has ever been able or will in the near future be able to write Flannery O'Connor or paint Vincent Van Gogh under the table. And as for being the delight of logicians, it was only when it finally dawned on me that I was not dealing with rational beings, but

[3]Maia Wojciechowska, "Who Should Write for Young Readers," *The Writer* (April 1971), p. 19.

with *children*, that I was able to summon the strength to survive motherhood.

Yet, it is not simply living with four members of this breed that keeps me from an idealistic view of childhood; it is the memory of myself as a child. I was not of the superior breed. Nor was I gifted or beautiful or free. I was scared and lonely and dumb. My vision of what I might be so far outstripped any reality that most of the time I hovered at the edge of despair. If I hadn't been so terrified, I might have fallen into the abyss. One of the positive uses of terror is that it is fairly time-consuming. As long as you're running about scared to death of life, you deny yourself the leisure demanded to contemplate despair.

Thus, when I write for the reader whose life I want to change, I am not writing for one of the beautiful people, but for one of the terrified—one of the "tired, the poor, the huddled masses, yearning to breathe free." If you must call me a didactic writer, go ahead. I do believe that those of us who have grown up have something of value to offer the young. And if that is didacticism, well, I have to live with it. But when I write a story, it is not an attempt to make children good or wise—nobody but God can do that, and even God doesn't do it without the child's coopera- tion. I am trying in a book simply to give children a place where they may find rest for their weary souls.

Let me explain. When I walk into a room full of well-dressed people, I never walk in alone. With me is a nine-year-old who knows her clothes are out of a missionary barrel, her accent is foreign, and her mannerisms peculiar—a child who knows that if she is lucky she will be ignored and if unlucky she will be sneered at. But the gift of maturity is this—not that I can ever excise that frightened, lonely nine-year-old or that I even want to, but that when I walk into that room I quickly recognize a hundred children just as fearful and desperate as I. And even if they are afraid to reach out to me, I can feel, along with my own nine-year-old loneliness, a kind of compassion, and make an attempt to reach out to them.

Flannery O'Connor was a gifted, isolated invalid, who never had children of her own, who never apparently even knew many children, but who remembered with the senses of the true artist what it was like to be a child. This is what she says:

> I was a very ancient twelve. My views at that age would have done credit to a Civil War Veteran. I'm much younger now than I was at twelve or anyway, less burdened. The weight of the centuries lies on children. I'm sure of it.[4]

The reader I want to change is that burdened child within myself. As I begin a book, I am in a way inviting her along to see if there might be some path through this wilderness that we might hack out together, some oasis in this desert where we might find refreshment, some sheltered spot where we might lay our burden down. This is done by means of a story—a story peopled by characters who are me but not simply me. And there is an element of mystery in the process. It is never a neat formula. For fiction has its own life, and the book that started to be mine, for myself, grows away from me and the child I was and becomes something quite apart from me.

Now having said all these very solemn and pompous things, I must stop and contradict myself. Although a work of entertainment may not be art, a work that intends to be art must first be entertaining. I have quoted one well-known writer on writing

[4]Flannery O'Connor, *The Habit of Being: Letters* (New York: Farrar, Straus, & Giroux, 1979), p. 137.

for children, now let me quote another—this is Anatole France
—less respectful perhaps, but with a valid point to make.

> It is much easier to write for men than for the little
> monkeys. One persuades men that it is the proper thing to
> read such and such a book. And they read it and praise it.
> When a child is bored, he tears the page and makes a paper
> doll or a boat.

And it's not just a matter of sticking in stuff to sweeten the pot, either. The whole story must entertain. In the words of the great master entertainer Charles Dickens: you must make them laugh, make them weep, but above all, make them wait. Somerset Maugham in *The Art of Fiction* makes the flat statement that ". . . the aim of art is to please." Surely, even in Caroline Gordon's description or F. R. Leavis's, the quality of pleasure, both emotional and intellectual, is not absent.

One of the questions that children continue to ask me in various guises is: "Do you know any real writers?" It is a question that those of us who pretend to be engaged in eternal enterprises need to have asked of us. And I must confess that nothing gives me the shudders quite so much as a review that suggests that my book is not for the ordinary child—but the special reader. If a book that I have written is only worth paper dolls and airplanes in the hands of ordinary children, then I had better give up and start writing for middle-aged ladies like myself. I do not mean that every child must like every book, but I do hope that many children of ordinary intelligence and sensibilities will enjoy reading what I have written. I was, after all, one of these children myself, carrying the weight of the world on very narrow shoulders.

51

There may be somewhere in this world children who carry no loads. The ones I know best wonder aloud at the supper table how nuclear waste can be disposed of, what to do about the starving, and whether to run away from home or take the math test that they have no hope of passing. After prayers have been said and the lights are out, they ask quietly in the darkness for assurance that their souls are not eternally damned and their bodies free of deadly cancers.

Perhaps only my children are so burdened. Perhaps it is a case of the sins of the mother being visited upon the next generation. But I do not think so. If it is only my children, why do I get letters from so many very ordinary children who recognize or claim to recognize their own pain in the stories I have told?

I cannot transmute their pain to joy, but I shall continue to try to provide a space where they can, if they wish, lay down a burden. I want them to know that despite all the evidence that the world seeks to crush them with, there is room for hope. That the good life, far from ending in childhood, barely begins there. That maturity is more to be desired than immaturity, knowledge than ignorance, understanding than confusion, perspective than self-absorption. That true innocence is not the absence of experience but the redemption of it.

LEARNING TO LOVE

❦

ALL TOGETHER NOW
by Sue Ellen Bridgers

When I read Sue Ellen Bridgers's first novel, *Home Before Dark*, it never occurred to me to ask for whom the book had been written. It was obviously written for me. Well, okay, for people like me, who want above all a really good story with characters they can care for deeply.

Sometime later I learned from a list in the library that *Home Before Dark* had not been published for me. The list categorized it as one of those shadowy entities known as the Young Adult Novel. I say "shadowy" because no one has explained to my satisfaction who, in book terms, is a young adult, much less what causes a book to carry the label. Something, I suppose— subject matter, style, an errant obscenity—may make a book not quite a children's book. But after that, why can't a novel just be a novel without tacked-on ages?

To be sure, *All Together Now*, Bridgers's second novel, begins with a twelve-year-old. Casey Flanagan has come to spend the summer with her grandparents while her father flies in the Korean War and her mother works two jobs to stave off fear and loneliness. The book starts with Casey's last summer as a child, yet it is not about emerging adolescence. Rather, it is, as the title suggests, a story of the members of an extended family reaching toward one another. It is a book about simple people learning how to love, and because love is a difficult task for the wisest of us, these simple people botch and bungle but never quite give up.

The book reminds me of a square dance with four couples: the various partners dance together and interact with the others in the square and then come home again. Jane and Ben Flanagan, Casey's paternal grandparents, are the head couple. It is against the solid harmony of their relationship that the other three pairs counter and clash and finally resolve. Casey's partner is Dwayne Perkins, a man her father's age who has been suspended in childhood ever since a porch swing broke, driving him headfirst into a wall. Couple number three are Casey's Uncle Taylor, working in his father's lumberyard but living for Saturday and the stock-car races, and Gwen, scooping popcorn and candy-covered raisins at the dime store and draping herself on a car hood to be watched at the races. Bridgers gently leads the reader from distaste to great concern for this five-and-dime romance between the peroxided clerk and the stock-car racer.

But the most fragile partnership, the one that makes the reader laugh and cry and wring her hands, is that of two friends of the Flanagan family. Bridgers's ability to create character is poignantly apparent in these two—the outwardly prim and meticulous Pansy, Jane's best friend from childhood, and the ex-traveling man and dancing waiter Hazard, who finally and disastrously dares to marry the doctor's aging daughter.

Learning to Love

In order to propel the reader into the center of this complex square, Bridgers has made a risky technical decision. She tells the story from the point of view of all of these eight people, sometimes switching point of view more than once on a single page. The reader is being asked to follow the intricate steps of the dance, and he may not always understand the calls. There is also, perhaps because of the frequent shifts in point of view, a consciousness of a presence behind that of the characters—not an intrusive nineteenth-century author-observer, to be sure— but a presence all the same. According to Flannery O'Connor it is always wrong "to say that you can't do this or you can't do that in fiction. You can do anything you can get away with, but nobody has ever gotten away with much." I hesitate to say then that a writer can't change points of view so often or enter into her own story. Bridgers has, and if she has not gotten clean away with it, she has certainly written a lovely book—a book for all of us who crave a good story about people we will come to care about deeply.

From THE WASHINGTON POST BOOK WORLD
(May 13, 1979)

YES, BUT IS IT TRUE?

A friend sent me recently a Miss Peach cartoon strip. At the left is a huge hand-lettered sign that says: "Arthur Answers the Eternal Questions," with a large arrow pointing toward Arthur, who is being questioned by a ponytailed seeker of wisdom. "Arthur," she asks, "is there anything worthwhile in life but truth and beauty?" "Yes," he replies, "there is love. Also, Chinese food." I do not need to tell you that the reason my friend sent me this cartoon is unrelated to my devotion to truth, beauty, and love. I am, in fact, distinctly uncomfortable in the face of eternal questions. Yet there is one eternal question which I as a writer of fiction for children and young people am often asked by children and never asked by adults.

"Is it true?" the child asks. "Is your story true?"

Ha! you say. We adults don't ask that question because we know you write *fiction*—and fiction "is the act of feigning or imagining that which does not exist or is not actual." Ergo—

fiction by definition is *not true.*

I'm being unfair. Some of you are wiser than that. And although you may never voice the question to the writer, you will come to one of my novels or to anyone's novel with that same question. Is it true?

And my answer for you is the same answer that I give the child who asks. "I hope so. I meant for it to be true. I tried hard to make it so."

I am a graduate of a small Presbyterian college. We had a college president who was a brilliant man full of aphorisms for every occasion. One of Dr. Liston's aphorisms has stuck with me through the years. It is this: "When the Greeks decided to get practical, they began running restaurants and shining shoes." By which I think he meant that civilization as well as education takes a downward spiral when it ceases to ask, "What is truth?" and concerns itself primarily with what is measurable.

In the beginning of all things was God, and in the beginning of human consciousness was the story. In an address to the Royal Society of Literature, Kipling once said that ". . . fiction is Truth's elder sister. Obviously! No one in the world knew what truth was till someone had told a story."

For proof of what Kipling says we need only to look at our own Biblical heritage and find that in the beginning there was the story. Perhaps the more orthodox among us would hesitate to say that it was the story that shaped the truth, but surely it has been the vehicle for the truth for as long as the human race can remember.

And such a delightful vehicle. It is almost a truism that the most exciting words in the English language are: "Once upon a time . . ." But for those of you who are suspicious of delight, let me remind you of the practical value of the story.

Bruno Bettelheim in his book *The Uses of Enchantment* advances the idea—which, though not original with him, is one that he, as a psychiatrist, eloquently champions—that the child who hears fairy tales is able to face the dark and wild side of his or her own nature and to comprehend on an unconscious level the incomprehensible adult world. Moreover, the fairy tale gives the child hope that he will succeed, overcoming the giants within and without—that he will live happily ever after.

Bettelheim does not feel that other kinds of stories have the same elemental power as the traditional fairy tale. This is a point I would want to argue, but the inarguable point is that stories will not have any power if they are never heard or read. Which brings me back to a concern about education. Why, in places of "higher learning," is the reading of fiction considered some kind of aberration? A recent issue of *Psychology Today* told about a student at Princeton University who finally transferred. He felt he was socially ostracized at Princeton because in his free time he would read novels.

You mustn't embarrass college students, much less college graduates, by asking them what novels they have read in the past year. And yet, for those who are seeking truth, which is nearer the truth, Stone and Church's statistically factual description of the average adolescent girl, or Tolstoy's picture of Natasha at the ball?

Fiction allows us to do something that nothing else quite does. It allows us to enter fully into the lives of other human beings. But, you may argue, these are not real people, they are fictitious —merely the figments of one writer's imagination. At this point, the other side of the brain takes over. There is nothing "mere" about Natasha. We know with what Walter de la Mare calls that "compelling inward ring" that Natasha is true. She is more real to us than the people we live with every day, because we have been allowed to eavesdrop on her soul.

A great novel is a kind of conversion experience. We come away from it changed. And just as a season with Natasha and André and Pierre may make us wiser and more compassionate people, a season with Heathcliff or Jude Fawley has the power to shake us at the roots. The fake characters we read about will evaporate like the morning dew, but the real ones, the true ones, will haunt us for the rest of our days.

We Christians have done a lot of preaching about sin—much of it incomprehensible and much of it doing nothing except laying on guilt and despair. Part of this is, I believe, because rational argument rarely convinces sinners and never saves them. But the other part is that everybody talking 'bout hell ain't a been there (to paraphrase the spiritual). Unlike our Lord, we have not been able or willing to descend into hell. So our words of grace seep out bland and bloodless. Perhaps this is why the tax collectors and harlots are closer to the kingdom of heaven than we.

But those of us who have followed Frodo on his quest have had a vision of the true darkness. We know that we, like him, would have never gotten up the steep slope of Mount Doom had the faithful Sam not flung us on his back and carried us up, crawling at the last. We know, too, that we would never have parted with the baneful ring of power had not the piteous Gollum torn it from our bleeding finger and, in the effort, fallen screeching into the abyss, clutching his damned treasure and ours.

When we read fiction that is true, we do not say, "There but for the grace of God go I"—rather, "Here I am." For in such writing we recognize our naked selves with a shudder or a laugh; sometimes, quite wonderfully, with both.

Over twenty years ago a college English professor said something that has bothered me ever since. He wondered aloud if it was possible to describe Christian experience effectively except by fantasy or science fiction. I've tried to fight this view, because I don't write fantasy or science fiction. But he may be right. I say this as one haunted by visions of the great lion Aslan, whose bright goodness never fails to flood my spirit with awe and joy.

I was once very much involved with a young man who, when I tried to share with him my love for C. S. Lewis's *Chronicles of Narnia*, said earnestly that he felt it was wrong of Lewis to distort the Bible in this way. I should have known at that moment that the relationship was doomed. Aslan is not a distortion but a powerful symbol of the Lion of Judah, which can nourish our spirits as the reasoned arguments of a thousand books of theology can never do. We can dare face the dark, because we've had a shining glimpse of the light.

If fiction is true for the reader of it, what about the writer? Is he or she out there laughing at those of us who have become so bewitched by the mere arrangement of words upon a page? I read recently that after Hardy had finished *Jude the Obscure* he never wrote another novel. He turned instead to writing poetry, so appalled, we may guess, by the vision of darkness he had created that he dared not go deeper into it himself.

So it can be a dangerous business. A friend of mine who writes history books said to me that he thought that the two creatures most to be pitied were the spider and the novelist—their lives hanging by a thread spun out of their own guts. But in some ways I think writers of fiction are the creatures most to be envied, because who else besides the spider is allowed to take that fragile thread and weave it into a pattern? What a gift of grace to be able to take the chaos from within and from it to create some semblance of order.

I only know one writer really well, and since she is the one making these observations, I must before I am through apply what I have been saying to her.

I can't tell you exactly when the story began, somewhere among the catacombs of childhood's fears, but it began to grow in the early months of 1974 along with a tumor, which, after a lifetime of blooming health, invaded my body. The cancer was removed, the prognosis hopeful, but by that time I had heard the bell toll. I could no longer pretend to be immortal. Before either I or my family had had time to recuperate from my illness, our David's closest friend, a winsome, humorous little girl of eight, was struck and killed by lightning. The two events were almost more than we could bear. Every time John or I left town, the children were sure we'd never return. I was known to wonder myself. David went through all the classical stages of grief and invented a few, including one in which he was sure that God was punishing him by killing off his loved ones, one by one. He had even worked out the order of demise. I was second on the list, right after his younger sister.

In the middle of all this I went to one of the regular monthly meetings of the Children's Book Guild in Washington. By some fluke I was seated at the head table with the guest speaker, who was Ann Durell, the editor for children's books at Dutton. During the polite amenities at the beginning of the meal, one of my fellow guild members said innocently, "How are the children?" To which, as you all know, the answer is "Fine." I muffed it. I began to really tell how the children were, which led me and my rather startled dinner mates into the long tale of David's grief.

When I finally shut up, the guest of honor said quietly, "I know this sounds just like an editor, but you ought to write that story." I thought I couldn't. The rule is, as you may know, that a writer should wait fifteen years before writing about an incident of personal history. It hadn't been five months. But I began to try. It became a way of dealing with my inability to comfort my child.

After many false starts I began to write a story in pencil in a used spiral notebook, so that if it came to nothing, I could pretend that I'd never been very serious about it. Gradually, I was encouraged by the emergence of thirty-two smudged pages to transfer from the tentative pencil to the typewriter, and the book moved forward, gathering momentum, only to become absolutely frozen. I found I couldn't let my fictional child die. I wrote around the death. I even cleaned the kitchen—anything to prevent this death from taking place.

Finally I confessed to a close friend of mine what was happening. "I guess I can't go through Lisa's death again," I concluded. She looked me straight in the eye. "I don't think it's Lisa's death you can't face, Katherine. I think it's yours."

Speaking of that "compelling inward ring." I went back to my study and closed the door. If it was Lisa's death I couldn't face, that was one thing, but if it was mine, by God, I would face it. I finished the chapter and, within a few weeks, the draft, with cold sweat rolling down my arms. And I did what no professional writer would ever do—I mailed it off to my editor before the sweat had evaporated.

I wish for every writer in the world an editor like Virginia

Buckley. She did not brush aside that fragile thread spun from my guts. "I laughed through the first two thirds," she told me, "and cried through the last." So it was all right. She understood, as she always has, what I was trying to do. But a thread is not a story, and in children's novels we still expect a story with a beginning, a middle, and an end. And this is what Virginia gently prodded me into weaving.

I love revisions. Where else in life can spilled milk be transformed into ice cream? We can't go back and revise our lives, but being allowed to go back and revise what we have written comes closest. By now I had some distance from the book. My heart had stopped pounding, my palms were dry, my head cool, and my eye cooler. I was far enough away from the facts to see the truth from which they sprang. I was now ready to write fiction.

If the early drafts had been conceived in fear and grief, this revision was born in joy. In the mere rearrangement of words upon a page, I had passed through a valley of the shadow and come out singing. In fact, when I sent Virginia the revision, I wrote her that I was sure love was blind, for I had just mailed her a flawless manuscript.

My vision, you'll be glad to know, has since been restored. I no longer believe that *Bridge to Terabithia* is without flaws. But to this day when a child asks me if it is true, I answer, trying not to tremble too conspicuously, "Oh, I hope so."

On 95, just before the Delaware line, there is a road sign I invariably look for. In the nearly fourteen years I've traveled that road, this one sign has been the high point of an otherwise monotonous superhighway. The sign reads: "Northeast Rising Sun." For years I had a fantasy that I would simply turn off the thruway at that point and drive until I found that Shangri-La—

that Brigadoon of Maryland named by an ancient poet, North-east Rising Sun. Then one day as I was smiling at my sign, a horrible thought struck. Suppose there was no such place? Suppose there was no village nestled in the eastern hills answering to that wonderful name? I didn't want to know, but that ubiquitous left side of my brain decided to ferret out the truth. I heard myself asking my husband, quite against my will, if it was possible that Northeast Rising Sun was not actually the name of a town. He was driving and entirely missed the quavering tone, replying very matter-of-factly that he thought it wasn't. Again, I let it lie. After all, husbands aren't always right, even mine. But the demon of brutal realism refused to give up. It drove me at last to a large map of the state and forced me to look in the northeast corner. Alas, as I had suspected, but was so long loath to acknowledge, there is no such place on the map as Northeast Rising Sun. There are, rather, two towns—Northeast on the east side of 95, and Rising Sun on the west. My poetic signboard was a fiction.

And fiction, though it may be true, is not *the* Truth any more than a signpost is a place. But it can be a signpost. Fiction is not the Gospel. But it can be a voice crying in the wilderness—and for the writer and the reader who know grace it will not be a cry of despair but a cry of hope—a voice crying in our wilderness: Prepare the way of the Lord.

A FAMILY OF STRANGERS

❧ ❦

THE DISAPPEARANCE
by Rosa Guy

Her publisher once said about Rosa Guy that her "literary themes stem from the fact that she is black and a woman." I suppose this kind of labeling is inevitable, but it is misleading. For a great strength of Guy's work is her ability to peel back society's labels and reveal beneath them highly individual men and women.

The Disappearance, her latest novel, brings together Imamu, a boy from the Harlem streets, the Aimsleys, a middle-class Brooklyn family, and their West Indian friends and neighbors. All of these people are black, which in no way diminishes the distance each must travel if he is to understand the others. Nor is there a single definition of womanhood. Imamu's wino mother; the immaculate, socially aware Ann Aimsley; the man-baiting Dora Belle; and Gail, a sheltered college student, spouting undigested liberal slogans—each is a carefully drawn character whose hidden strengths and weaknesses have the power to heal or to destroy. Imamu has cause to fear each one of them, and they, him.

This is a story about fear and its tragic consequences. Not just the fear of the powerless black in an unfeeling or cruel white society, but the myriad fears that cause black persons to mistrust and hurt each other. Ann Aimsley, in a seemingly brave and selfless gesture, rescues Imamu from the juvenile court system and determines to make him her foster son. Her husband, who fought his own way up from the streets, is openly antagonistic. Her daughter Gail is torn between physical attraction to the tall, arrogant youth and discomfort in his presence. The only member of the family who can accept the newcomer without fear is eight-year-old Perk, and she disappears the day after Imamu joins the family.

Imamu is immediately suspect. Despite or because of the fact that the elder Aimsleys and their West Indian friend Dora Belle turn him over to the police to be interrogated and beaten, Imamu determines to find Perk. And Gail, stunned by her parents' and godmother's betrayal of the boy, joins him in searching for her lost sister.

The book deepens now into a tale of suspense with something of a love story to round it off.

The image Guy uses to bind these disparate elements is a painting, which hangs over the Aimsleys' couch and was painted by a former boarder who left it behind for unpaid rent. At first glance, it appears to be simply a picture of a storm at sea. But as Imamu studies it, he realizes that what he took for shadow under the foam is, in fact, hundreds of tiny matchstick bodies being crushed by the wave. In a scene that leads directly to his solving the mystery of Perk's disappearance, he is looking once more at the painting.

"He could see that for those spinning around like matchsticks in the whirlpool, with not even a toehold in the sand, there was a sense of terror and of pleasure on their faces at the same time—adding up to intense relief at being sucked in, giving in to the forces bent on crushing them into that mass.

"Imamu felt the pull, the terror, the pleasure of giving in. *Then he knew!* He was looking at the results. Nevertheless, his feet ached to take off, his body to be sucked in. . . . Yet he had to struggle . . . struggle . . . struggle. . . ."

This is a harsh book, but not a hopeless one. It is a book that cries to its readers to resist being sucked in—crushing and being crushed—but it is not a polemic. For Rosa Guy, the writer, is not primarily a black or a woman, but one of that rare and wonderful breed, a storyteller. May her tribe increase.

From THE WASHINGTON POST BOOK WORLD
(November 11, 1979)

THE PERILOUS REALM
OF REALISM

❧ ❦

Since people have begun to ask my opinion about things, they, especially librarians, want to know who my own favorite writers for children are. I never seem to be prepared for this question, and I'm sure I give different names whenever I am asked. Last year in Baltimore, I found myself taking the time to give a really nice long list. There is, as you know, a lot of good writing being done for children and young people these days, and though I haven't read it all, it's not for want of trying. When I had finished my list, someone piped up. "Do you realize," she asked, "how top-heavy that list is with fantasy writers?" I hadn't realized it before, being living proof that the unexamined life is quite worth living. But of course these librarians wanted me to explain the significance of it all, since I myself was not a writer of fantasy.

What it means, I suppose, is that deep down within myself I believe that the *real* writers are the poets and that crowding the poets in the hierarchy of literature are the fantasists. You'll notice that when my characters read books they tend to read fantasy—fairy tales or C.S. Lewis or Tolkien. And, as an aside, there was some discussion with my editor about a number of literary allusions in *Bridge to Terabithia*. She didn't mind, but would they bother children who hadn't read the books? My feeling was that it ought to bother them so much that they'd rush out and get the books and read them. I was absolutely delighted when a fifth grader asked me shyly if that remark on page 57 about the assistant pig keeper meant that Jesse was reading *The Book of Three*, which was obviously one of her favorite books.

I realize that it is very logical to ask why, if I like fantasy so much, I am not writing it. Or, for that matter, why I'm not writing poetry. Well, I doubt that many writers say: "Hereto I will write me a fantasy, or I will write me a bit of realism." A story occurs to you, and you are well into dealing with it before you start analyzing what genre you're involved with. If a great tale of fantasy came to me, I'd rush to write it down. But I can't imagine sitting down before my typewriter and saying: "Today is the day I'm going to write fantasy."

The closest I have ever come to writing fantasy was in the early drafts of *Bridge to Terabithia*. In order to show the reader that Terabithia was for Jess and Leslie a magical kingdom, I switched to a more formal language, resembling, as I thought, that which occurs in tales of high fantasy. I should like to quote my editor's reaction.

> . . . The idea of the Terabithia secret place is very good, though the scenes themselves are a little weak. The style of the writing changes noticeably, and this can be seen

especially on page 35. This aspect of the story is what needs strengthening the most. I think it might be difficult for children to attain the same elevated dreamland each time that they enter into the magic kingdom. The greater magic might be in what is happening in their relationship. . . .

Needless to say, my formal language of fantasy went out the nearest window. It had not worked.

Yet as I talk to children about this book, I find that something has happened for which I cannot take credit. They have taken my bare-bones Terabithia and supplied their own fantasies. I received from a class a sheaf of pictures of Terabithia— magnificent castles with drawbridges, knights in armor—all the trappings of high fantasy. In a listing for teachers and librarians the book was described as "a realistic narrative with overtones of fantasy." Even my adult readers seemed to be doing it. Once I had pitched out my pretentious passages and told in simple language what was happening between two children, readers young and old brought their own fantasies to the book. I could not count the number of people who have told me that Terabithia is exactly like a magical place they have or had when they were children. But, of course, what has happened is that they have made Terabithia in their own image. I didn't write the book. They did. It's an absolutely wonderful experience for a writer to have people do this. If I knew how to make it happen, believe me, I'd put it up in mason jars against those long hard winters ahead.

Yet as satisfying to the writer in me as this is, the reader in me has the uncomfortable feeling that she doesn't know exactly what the terms "fantasy" and "realism" mean in the strictly literary sense. At such times, I turn to my trusty twin references, *The Oxford Companion to American Literature* and *The Oxford Companion to English Literature.*

I find to my great shock that neither volume so much as mentions fantasy. It may be significant that these particular editions date back to my youth and that this scandalous omission has by now been corrected, or it may be that fantasy was far too clever and lively to sit around waiting to be netted and chloroformed and stuck through with a pin for people to stare at. Maybe it saw how those people had treated realism and took flight. "Also in the arts," says the *Oxford Companion to English Literature,* "a loosely used term meaning truth to the observed facts of life (especially when they are gloomy)." Who would blame fantasy for not wanting to be referred to as a "loosely used term"? It doesn't sound respectable somehow.

However, I must admit, if somewhat grumpily, that there are grounds for referring to realism as a "loosely used term." What is true to the observed facts of one person's life would be fantasy to another's. In the days when I had published only historical fiction, I used to be roundly taken to task for not writing "true-to-life stories" that today's children could identify with.

It seemed to me then, and I must say, still does, that in many instances historical fiction is a heap sight more realistic than a lot of today's "realism." I find it very strange when people separate realistic from historical (by which they seem to mean romantic and therefore unrealistic) fiction. Nothing becomes dated more quickly than certain contemporary fiction, which then of course seems most unrealistic to the young reader. Anything, as you know, that takes place before a child's own immediate memory seems to the child ancient and exotic. My own children have the perfect phrase to describe this phenomenon. "Back when you were alive, Mom . . ." Some writers try to avoid this dating process, so that when you read their books you are struck by the lack of anchors to the real world. There is no date, no description of clothing or current events, no slang. How could you call such a book, even loosely, "true to the facts of observed life"?

In contrast, in historical novels, the writer is free to anchor her characters with every fact of life she wants to use—the only limit being on details that would impede the progress of the story and therefore drive off all but the most doggedly determined of readers.

When I first began to write historical fiction, I had no idea that it was a sort of bastard child of letters—respectable neither as history nor as fiction. Twelfth-century Japan, torn apart by wasteful wars and civil strife, didn't seem very far away from Washington, D. C., in the late 1960's. It never occurred to me that I was writing romantic literature. It seemed not only realistic but terrifyingly current.

Historical fiction has its own perils. A friend, a middle-aged American businessman, who read *The Sign of the Chrysanthemum*, made a point of telling me at church one Sunday how much he had enjoyed the book. He hadn't really expected to, knowing nothing of ancient Japan, but the thing he had found quite wonderful was how those ancient Japanese, eight hundred years and half a world away, thought as he did—the same dreams and fears. "People don't change, do they?" he concluded.

I stammered for an answer. The dreams and fears of the ancient Japanese as revealed in their own literature from the twelfth century are indeed recognizable to us as the dreams and fears of fellow human beings, but the dreams and fears of the characters in *The Sign of the Chrysanthemum* belonged to the middle-aged American housewife he was talking to. And struggle as I will to make each of my historical novels true and realistic to its own time, I do not forget that it is my twentieth-century Western mind that sifts those faraway events and introduces to the reader the characters who allegedly took part in them. My books are not Japanese novels. They are Western novels about Japan.

So while in being true to the times and feelings of feudal Japan I will relate to my reader cruelties that may be absent from much contemporary fiction for young people, there are things, quite true things, that I haven't written about and probably shall not, because I cannot find a way to do so within the boundaries of my own moral code.

I long, for example, to write a fictionalized biography of Yoshitsune, the great romantic hero of the Gempei Wars, but Yoshitsune died a ritual suicide. I cannot bring myself to seem to glorify suicide, which shows how far my mind is from the mind of a twelfth-century Japanese warrior. The closest I have come to dealing with suicide for the sake of honor is the scene in *Of Nightingales that Weep* that takes place at the battle of Dannoura. And then, you notice, I would not allow Takiko to jump off the ship. She, being Japanese and the daughter of a samurai, had to regret her cowardice. I did not.

Being true to the facts of history has certain limitations for a writer, but I must confess a rather obvious advantage. Historical facts offer all kinds of help in that devilish task of plotting a story. In *The Master Puppeteer*, for example, the story is stretched between the plague of 1773 (during which 200,000 are said to have died) and the great famine of Tokugawa times, which began in 1783 and lasted until 1787, with food riots erupting in all the major Japanese cities toward its end—a thirteen- to fourteen-year period, the entire lifetime of a young adolescent.

Now Jiro with his drive for perfection, which he cannot of course satisfy, his impulsiveness, his ambition, his loyalty to his friends is a person I know very well. But there are parts of Jiro that are not true to the facts of life as I know them, that I must imagine. How would being born in a year when hundreds of thousands are dying affect how his parents felt about him? How, in turn, would he come to feel about himself? How would living on the edge of starvation affect a boy as he entered the period of his life when enormous amounts of food are needed to fuel adolescent growth and energy? How would his life and the lives of those he cares for be affected by a city in which the oppressed finally explode in self-destructive rage?

In choosing to tell such a story, I saw that a certain honesty was demanded by history. I could no more prettify the riots of Osaka than I could the riots of Watts or Detroit or Washington. Readers have recoiled from the maiming of Kinshi. The authorities were cruel in eighteenth-century Japan. But during the riots that occurred in Washington just over ten years ago, there were many voices demanding that the police shoot to kill all looters or *would-be looters*. Perhaps we haven't moved quite so far from the ancient cruelties as we'd like to think we have.

Perhaps if I can understand why the poor of Osaka felt driven to senseless violence, I will be driven to examine the roots of violence in my own city. Recently my husband was called to the aid of an elderly widow who had a total monthly income of $205, from which she had to hand over $189 to a landlord who lived, as I imagined him, quite comfortably and peacefully in a distant suburb, totally oblivious to the violence that he was inflicting on another human life. Perhaps a reader, though this may be too much to ask, reading of the rice merchants of Osaka, will recognize his own unconscious complicity in the acts of violence committed daily against the poor of the world. But if not the reader, surely the writer.

If the question is "Realistic for whom?" the answer must be "Realistic for me." I cannot pretend to know what is real for someone else. I can only be true to the observed facts of my own life.

I suppose I am most aware of this in the creation of characters. People often ask if this character or another is a "real person." Of course, I hope they're all real people. I would hope so even if they were animals or fairy folk. But that is not what the questioner means. He means, did I see this guy walking around one day or did I make him up? In addition, when some people hear that I have four children, they say, "What marvelous material for your books," as though my husband and I had collected children instead of encyclopedias. The children in my books are not thinly disguised members of my family. But I haven't been able to convince my children of this.

When *Bridge to Terabithia* was still a pile of messy papers on my desk, my son John began sneaking in to read it. We both pretended that I didn't know what he was up to, until one day he burst into the kitchen, perfectly furious. "That boy started out being me and now he's turned into David!" he said. The truth of the matter is that if Jesse Aarons is modeled, except in superficial ways, after any real person, it is not either of my sons, but me. It is my thoughts and insecurities and especially my fears that Jess possesses.

Even more startling than John's fury over Jesse Aarons was our daughter Mary's remark: "I can't figure out who my William Ernest is." It was one of those times when I could not understand what was being said. "Mary"—I could hardly believe it—"do you think Gilly is supposed to be you?"

"Sure," she said. "I just can't figure out who my William Ernest is."

Now Gilly Hopkins is a skinny, chop-haired blonde, sassy, bigoted, obnoxious, whose great delight is making life miserable for her weird little foster brother, whose name is William Ernest. My daughter Mary is a sturdy, dark-haired Apache-Kiowan with one of the most sensitive, loving natures I've ever met in a fellow human being. I tried my best to convince my daughter that I had never for one moment thought of her as a big-mouthed bully who took malicious delight in scaring the wits out of the little William Ernests of the world. But Mary refused to be persuaded. She wanted to be Gilly or for Gilly to be her. She wasn't about to be robbed of the privilege by the fevered protests of Gilly's creator.

I was reminded of a wonderful article on writing by Anne Tyler, in which she says:

> I write because I want more than one life; I insist on a wider selection. It's greed plain and simple. When my characters join the circus, I'm joining the circus. Although I'm happily married, I spend a great deal of my time mentally living with incompatible husbands.[1]

Perhaps the reason I tried so hard to persuade my daughter that she was not the great Gilly Hopkins was because I wanted to be. I'm greedy. I want to be them all. In psychology this is known, I believe, as fantasizing.

But looking back, I don't seem to have ever created a character that some corner of my soul does not personally claim—from the rogue samurai Takanobu to Monster Mouth Myers. I am all

[1] Anne Tyler, "Because I Want More Than One Life," *The Washington Post* (August 15, 1976).

of them—the wily Saburo as well as the fearful Jesse. A character may be a confession of secret sin or a revelation of hidden longings, but my fantasies are as much me as is my public face, and all my characters are as true, therefore, to the facts of my life as I have the skill to make them.

This is what realism in fiction is about, it seems to me. Another of my many dictionaries defines it as "fidelity to nature or to real life." And although some may interpret this as faithfulness to sordid, minute, gloomy detail, it seems to me that the faithfulness we are talking about is faithfulness to the human spirit in all its aspects. Fantasy becomes real when the characters, human or otherwise, reflect human nature as we know it. Not just human nature as a general blob, either, for the acts and thoughts of a created character must ring true for that particular character. If it is the universals that provide us with a point of identification, it is surely the particulars that make us want to identify. We don't identify with Everyman, but with Natasha and Huck Finn and Ramona Quimby.

As a writer, it is in discovering the particularities of my characters that they cease to be me and begin to grow into themselves. It is easy to describe the parts of a character that are me, but the parts that are not me demand research and observation. And if these particularities ring false I am in deep trouble, like Poo Bah in *The Mikado*, whose particularities you'll recall were "merely corroborative detail intended to give artistic verisimilitude to an otherwise bald and unconvincing tale." Poo Bah was nearly boiled in oil for his corroborative details. There should be a moral in there somewhere.

But Poo Bah was on the right track. The actual facts of life tend to serve up many a "bald and unconvincing tale." But perhaps "bald" is not the word, since life tends to be as chock-full and disorderly as the city dump. The writer of realistic fiction is not a steam-shovel operator but a treasure hunter. In finding the story, a great deal of garbage will have to be sifted through and discarded.

Once more let me quote Anne Tyler. This is from her *Washington Post* review of Margaret Drabble's *Ice Age*.

> . . . With its accuracy and its wealth of detail, it is unerringly true to life, but in the very best sense it is *untrue* to life; it tells us more than we would ever find out in reality; it tells us less, by just the right amount, than what we would like to know.[2]

If you think of realism as a perilous realm to be transversed, here is a chart. We who would write realistic novels must find the path that goes between what is true to life and what "in the very best sense is untrue to life." By allowing our readers into the soul of a character we are letting them know more than life will ever divulge about another human being. But we must stop short of telling all. Not only must we guide them safely around the bogs of boredom and the sloughs of despond that will suck them in and lose them to us forever, but we must ensure them the great open spaces they need to set their own imaginations soaring.

[2] Anne Tyler, "Rank Smell of Success," *The Washington Post Book World* (October 10, 1977).

78

ATHENS TO SPARTA

❧ ❧

CHILDREN OF THE FOX
by Jill Paton Walsh

Jill Paton Walsh, author of *Goldengrove* and *Unleaving*, has never been content to plunk down upon her well-earned laurels and grind out more of the same. *Children of the Fox* proves it. The book is neither a novel nor a story collection. I tried the word triptych, but that implies that these three stories are simply hinged together. It does not convey the daring architecture that Paton Walsh has chosen to employ in constructing this book.

As I began reading, I was quickly caught up in a story of Aster, an Athenian girl, who risks her honor to go to Themistokles, the Greek general known as "the fox," to report what appears to be treachery. It is not, in fact, treachery at all but a clever trap, which Themistokles has set for the Persians. Aster is enlisted to keep the secret.

Eager to see how the high-spirited Aster will manage as a proper Greek wife, I turned to the next section, but Aster had disappeared. In her place, telling his story, was the goat-herding son of a wounded veteran whose olive groves have been destroyed by the retreating Persians. I was annoyed. How dare the author get me all caught up in Aster's life only to pluck me up and drop me smack in the middle of another?

Soon, however, it was Demeas who claimed my concern as he retraced the route of the original Marathon to carry news from Athens to Themistokles in Sparta. I am not a runner, but you don't have to be one to take delight in Paton Walsh's descriptions of the landscape Demeas is running through.

I left Demeas planting his new olive grove and entered a hideout on a mountainside built by two children of the Molosian king. Concealed from both Spartan and Athenian searching parties in the children's cleverly constructed play place is Themistokles, seen as a hunted fox.

Gradually I began to catch on. The book is not meant to be about the children, at least not primarily. The book is about the fox. But Walsh never lets us view Themistokles directly; we must grow to know him through the stories of the children whose lives touch his. It is a stunning way to present a character as well as an intriguing way to capture a period of history. Only a writer of Paton Walsh's skill could pull it off at all, and I am not sure she has totally succeeded, though my very chafing at the switch from one child to the next may be a backward compliment. The end effect is a book that sent me straight to Thucydides' *The Peloponnesian War*. I can't remember the last time a work of historical fiction made me rush to the library for the primary sources.

Historical fiction should first of all be true to its setting. *Children of the Fox* certainly is, but it goes beyond that. The story of Greece 2,500 years ago becomes, quite subtly in Paton Walsh's hands, a story of our own time. We, like Aster, Demeas, and

Lalla have puzzled over the machinations of rulers and generals. Few of us are wise enough to see to the core of any current crisis. Democracies still seem to breed a certain fickleness toward their heroes, and politics through the millennia has made strange bedfellows. Why, asks Aster, is Themistokles urging the Persians to attack his army? Why, asks Demeas, has Themistokles made Pausanias of Sparta a party to Athens' most closely kept secret? But the most ironic question is that posed by the barbarian princess Lalla, who has helped Themistokles escape from Greece:

> ". . . put aside your writing things, and walk with me, and begin my education for me by explaining something to me I would very much like to understand. Themistokles won a great victory for Athens, didn't he? And on the Great King he inflicted a bitter defeat. Yet the Athenians drove him out, and the Great King has given him three cities. . . . So tell me, how can it be that men love Athens? What kind of a city can it be? Themistokles, I am sure must hate it now."
>
> "Young mistress," said the Athenian, "when you see Themistokles among the barbarians, ask him if he hates Athens; ask him if he would not rather be at home."

True patriotism, as Paton Walsh understands, is a more mysterious passion than romantic love. For why should Themistokles, or Boris Pasternak, or Eldridge Cleaver, or even I, having seen the evil and folly of our countries, still love them? And yet we do. I closed the book not only an admirer of the fox but one of his kin.

From THE WASHINGTON POST BOOK WORLD
(July 9, 1978)

IN SEARCH OF A STORY

The Setting as Source

Last year's obituaries for Agatha Christie seemed apologetic for the fact that Dame Agatha's powers lay in her ability to construct ingenious plots. The implication was that great writers are strong on theme and character, and even setting, but plot is somewhat beneath them. Yet the truth of the matter is that the reason Agatha Christie is known and loved and bought by millions is that the answer to the question: "Who cares who killed Roger Ackroyd?" is: We all do, or nearly all of us do. We care desperately.

I am one of the plebeian mass who really care. I love stories. I am devoted to stories. I feel sure that at three I did not ask "Why?" but rather, "*Then* what happened?" The reason I began to write fiction was not that I believed myself to be one of those enviable artists, the "born storyteller," but that I loved stories so much I wanted to be on the inside.

Unfortunately, loving stories is not necessarily being able to write them. This was the first hard lesson I had to learn, which explains why there is still a file drawer in my study full of unpublished manuscripts. It may also explain why I turned to historical fiction, for I discovered that a historical setting provides a rich warp for a writer's woof.

I had thus completed two novels for young people set in twelfth-century Japan and was casting about for an idea for a third novel, when I made the mistake of asking my children what kind of book they would like. "You ought to write a mystery story," they said. I was horrified. They obviously didn't realize how hard plotting had always been for me. "Don't you know," I said, "what kind of brain it takes to plan and execute a mystery story?" I reminded them that Lin, our oldest, had been beating me consistently at chess since she was six. How could a mind that couldn't plot chess moves plot a mystery?

A few mornings later, a face glared out at me from the entertainment section of *The Washington Post*. It was that of a Japanese warrior puppet. Bunraku, the classical Japanese puppet theater, was coming to the Kennedy Center.

It had been fifteen years since the first time I had seen Bunraku in a small, dark theater in Osaka. The audience that day was made up almost entirely of little old ladies in black kimonos, and the homely smell of rice and fish and soy sauce rose from their wooden lunch boxes to permeate the theater. But when I looked at the stage, I was swept into another world. There the large, gorgeously arrayed puppets played out one of the countless stories about the forty-seven faithful retainers who spent their lives avenging the disgrace and death of their lord. The puppets, each flawlessly manipulated by three operators, seemed almost to come alive. It was the "almost" that sent a little thrill of fear through me as I remembered Bunraku. There was something sinister about the puppets, so close to life, but not quite alive, shadowed by the hooded forms of the manipulators—the perfect setting for a mystery story, if one could write a mystery story.

Since I was convinced that I could not, the whole idea would have been folded up and put out with the papers, except that my memory of the theater, once aroused, refused to be disposed of. A week or so later, I came half awake in the middle of the night with a scene playing in my head. I was looking into the upper floor of an old Japanese storehouse. By the light of the one tiny window I could see a boy, scrabbling about in the semi-darkness. From the panicked way he was searching, I guessed both that he had no business being there in the storehouse and that the thing he was looking for was not where he had expected it to be. As I watched the frantic boy, wondering who he was and what he was looking for, I heard a *thump, thump, thump* on the stairs. Both the boy and I turned at the sound. In the gloom at the head of the stairs, there appeared the white face of a warrior puppet, at its hand, the flash of a sword blade. Behind the puppet, almost eclipsed in shadow, was the hooded form of a single puppeteer. End of scene.

By this time, needless to say, I was fully awake, beating my brain. Who was the boy? What was he looking for in the forbidden storehouse? And who was the hooded manipulator menacing him through a puppet? But, alas, the subconscious that had served up a puzzle gratis was not about to hand me a plot free of charge. I was going to have to write the book myself and find out. So I went to the place I'd been to before—I went to a setting in search of a story.

People like to ask historical novelists about their research. For me the kind of research they are talking about comes later; first I have to search the setting for the warp of my story. Setting for me is not a background against which a story is played out, but the very stuff with which the story will be woven. The characters will not determine the setting, but the setting to a great extent will determine both what they will be like and how they will act.

For this book, then, there were two rich areas to be explored. The first was that of the puppet theater itself, a highly, and, often in the past, harshly, disciplined world where the individual must be willing to sacrifice everything for the demands of his art. The other was the late eighteenth-century city of Osaka, ravaged by plague and famine and torn by civil disorder. Already the setting had given me a dramatic contrast—the absolute order of the puppet theater and the chaos outside its gates.

It was the characters who had to bring the two together. The conflict had to take place within them. So the boy I had glimpsed in the storehouse became the hungry son of a puppet maker who apprenticed himself to the one place in Osaka where he thought he might get plenty of food. This immediately posed another puzzle. Why would there be plenty of food in the puppet theater?

History gave me an obvious answer. The rice merchants and moneylenders of the city were making huge profits while the masses starved. These greedy men were still going to the theater and paying to get in—an obvious answer, but hardly one that contributed to the excitement of my story. For, you see, I had gotten reckless and promised my children to write, not a true mystery, but at least an adventure story with plenty of suspense. Just how much adventure could I wring from box-office receipts? No, there had to be another answer. Perhaps a person who resented the exploitation of the poor as much as I did— someone who might want to take justice into his own hands.

Saburo the bandit is not based on a historical figure, although, as you devotees of samurai films well know, Japanese tradition abounds with tales of clever rogues who outwit the powerful to give succor to the weak. But the Saburo I was beginning to know was not the character so often played by Toshiro Mifune, a rude and engaging renegade whose deviling of the authorities the audience greets with guffaws and cheers. My bandit would have something of the bravado of a Robin Hood and the shrewdness of a Scarlet Pimpernel, but there was in him an element that set him apart from these hero rogues. Coming as he did, out of puppetry, Saburo would be a manipulator—a puppeteer of human lives—the sort of man, however marvelous, of whom it is well to be wary.

The setting also began to shape Jiro, the name, meaning simply "second son," which I had given my young apprentice. In searching out his history, I discovered that to have been thirteen at the climax of the Temmei famine, Jiro would have been born in a year of plague that claimed 200,000 lives.

It's hard to remember from this vantage point in what order the pieces began to tumble into position, as each answer led to another question. If he was the second son, what had happened to the first? He must, of course, have died of plague. How, then, had Jiro's parents reacted to his birth at so terrible a time? How had the long battle against starvation affected them? A scrawny, bitter woman began to emerge. Her one surviving child would not be able to understand her, even the scrap of humor she had managed to salvage from adversity would be lost on him. But I am an imperfect mother myself, and I longed for someone full of life and humor to rescue her from herself and teach her guilt-ridden son to care for her. Someone who was, nonetheless, helpless to understand his own stern father, whose inscrutable behavior was tied somehow to the central question of the book—the identity of Saburo the bandit.

There are magical moments in writing historical fiction when the woof of one's invention moving through the warp of history suddenly seems to make sense. The pattern begins to emerge, filling the writer with surprise and joy. One such moment of ecstasy makes all the plodding hours fall away.

I kept waiting for my moments. Chapter after chapter I posed and answered questions. I jammed pieces into place, only to reread what I had written with leaden despair. From the richest material I'd ever worked with, I was painstakingly producing an absolute contradiction in terms—a dull adventure story.

Only pride kept me going. My publishers had doubled the advance on my second novel to allow me to go to Osaka to research this one. My husband had managed the household and cared for the three children I had left behind for the three weeks our older daughter and I had spent in Japan. The Bunraku people in Osaka had given me hours of their time, patiently explaining their knowledge and art. If the book for which so many people had given so much never came into being, how could I ever face them? And then, too, I had promised the children.

But I was sick. As it turned out, literally. My husband prodded and nagged me into finishing the hated draft before I went into the hospital, at which time I put it aside and turned my attention to the kinds of questions the removal of a cancerous tumor posed.

Three months later our family was vacationing as usual in the barn that we rent in the Adirondacks. I wasn't feeling up to tennis, but I did feel brave enough at last to take another look at my dead story and see if there was any hope of its ever coming to life. I began to revise, little by little. It was obvious that no single operation would cure it, but time had given me distance. It didn't seem the overwhelming failure it had seemed before. I began to believe that my physical condition had not only affected my earlier work but also my opinion of it. Now that I was feeling better, so was the manuscript.

One night an electrical storm knocked out our lights. In a cabin in the woods, it is very dark when the lights go out. The children were restless and apprehensive, so we lit candles and I began to read the story out loud. As I did, I heard bumps in the rhythm that needed smoothing, and when I had failed to make some exotic detail clear, the audience stopped me and made me explain. I dared feel a faint hope.

The next day I found John, who was ten, going through the desk, looking for the manuscript. He couldn't wait until night to find out what happened next. The hope burst into flame. I knew, at last, that I had a story.

It was more than a year before the book was actually published. After the family editors passed on it, there was still my editor at Crowell, Virginia Buckley, who pointed out, among other things, that the scene in the storehouse, though "clever and terrifying," didn't work. I should have been warned that the scene one clings to most is very likely the one that needs lopping off, but I chose to retain it and rewrite in an attempt to make it grow more organically from what came before it. Artistically, I've never been absolutely sure it works even yet, but it's the one scene that my young readers have relished, so I'm glad it's there. Two Japanese experts read the manuscript and suggested corrections, gently chiding me for committing the cardinal sin of Japanese puppetry. In Bunraku, the puppeteers must be the "shadows of the dolls." My puppeteers were obviously overshadowing their puppets.

At last it was done, the adventure story that I had promised the children, but when I looked at it closely, I realized that the setting had given me more than a simple adventure story. It had given me a plea for justice and compassion. There it was woven through the whole pattern. I hope the children see it.

From THE WRITER
(April 1978)

NOT FOR CHILDREN ONLY

ABSOLUTE ZERO
Being the Second Part of the Bagthorpe Saga
by Helen Cresswell

Watching the March snowfall, my mood matched the patches of grayish ice that had lain for months under the azalea bushes. I began to read a book that the flap copy was recklessly trumpeting as a "side-splitting romp." Knowing the fragility of humor, I was quite aware that it was the wrong moment for such a book, but there was no help for it. Through clenched teeth, I dared the author to split my sides, and began.

Absolute Zero, as I was soon forced to admit, begins well. Uncle Parker, related only by marriage to the multitalented and poli-eccentric Bagthorpes, has won a slogan contest for "Sugar-Coated Puffballs," which entitles him and his wife Celia (who writes poetry and pots) to a cruise in the Caribbean. By the end of Chapter One, the fiercely jealous clan are feverishly entering every competition in the British Isles. Before long the prizes, some rather more welcome than others, begin pouring in.

The plot of this book, even more than that of the first volume in the saga, *Ordinary Jack*, defies description. I would sound like one of my children relating a Marx Brothers movie. But the plot is not by any means the only thing that makes this a very funny book. Yes, funny, even hilarious. For there I sat, laughing out loud in my cold, dark, empty house, while the giant snowflakes falling outside my window not only continued but clung glumly to the wet ground.

The characters are marvelous, from Grandma Bag, who cannot bear to lose at anything, even if the result is a Bingo Hall riot, to four-year-old Daisy, a reformed pyromaniac. It is, however, a good thing that we met the family in *Ordinary Jack,* for in this volume no one stands around long enough to be introduced. Except perhaps Zero, Jack's pudding-footed, mutton-headed mongrel, who has only been known to move rapidly on those several occasions when the house has caught fire. In this book, incidentally, Zero becomes the most celebrated and photographed dog in all of England.

Now a wild plot peopled by a family more harebrained than the Vanderhofs of *You Can't Take it With You* ought to be enough of a romp for any reader, young or old, but the quality in Helen Cresswell's books that will charm a laugh out from between clenched teeth is her mastery of language. She has that Thurber-like ability to harness words and syntax for a fully satisfying comic effect.

The proper thing for a reviewer to do at this point is to quote a line or two to prove the point. Sorry, but it can't be done. Cresswell's books don't cut up into neat quotable snippets. A part of what makes them funny is the cumulative effect, not only of several pages, or chapters, but of the two books, read in sequence. And one reason *Absolute Zero* may seem funnier than *Ordinary Jack* is this great snowballing of humorous events and phrases through the course of both volumes. At this rate, Volume Three will do us all in.

If Helen Cresswell's considerable talent is unknown to many American readers, it is not because she herself is a new writer. She has published more than fifty books for children, three of which have been runners-up for Britain's prestigious Carnegie Medal. A fair number of these books, many of them fantasies, have been published in this country. But if her American audience has been relatively narrow until now, "The Bagthorpe Saga" should remedy that. Everyone loves really funny books, don't they?

But, you ask, how many American children will understand, much less appreciate, Cresswell's very British brand of humor? Isn't humor the most fragile of literary commodities, the one most likely to perish in transition? Anticipating this question, I asked my thirteen-year-old to read the books. I can report that at least one All-American Boy found himself laughing out loud at *Ordinary Jack*—which was a problem, actually, because he was sneak-reading after lights-out and didn't want to be discovered. His report on *Absolute Zero* confirms my own opinion that it is even funnier. When I asked him how old a person would have to be to enjoy the books, he said that he thought children younger than he might have trouble catching on.

My feeling is that the plot and characters are strong enough to delight younger children who might not, as John suggests, catch on to the batting about of literary allusions, but there is plenty of humor for all. It would be a great series of books to read aloud. And as for catching on to all the jokes—I found myself,

Not for Children Only

magnifying glass in hand, poring over the small print of my compact edition of the *Oxford English Dictionary* to find the definition of "absolute zero." I suspect Cresswell's tucked another joke in there, and I hate to miss even one.

From THE WASHINGTON POST BOOK WORLD
(April 9, 1978)

LAYING THE FIRST PLANK

My mother used to say that anyone who could read should never try to clean. I think of this every time I try to clean my study. No scrap of paper can be thrown away without a careful reading. It does tend to ensure lack of progress, but, as the Japanese say, *Shikataganai*. There ain't nothing you can do about it.

I was engaged in this futile activity in late December of 1978. We were to move to Norfolk the next month, after thirteen years in Maryland, and I was determined to leave some of the trash behind. In my bulging file I came across a three-page draft of something that looked vaguely familiar. As I read it, the memory started my pulse thumping in my temple. It was the first plank of *Bridge to Terabithia*.

After I had decided to try to write some story growing out of David and Lisa's friendship, I sat down at the typewriter and for days nothing happened. Finally, I said to myself: "Okay. If you can't write what you want to, write what you can." So I wrote three pages, promptly lost them for three years, and didn't even remember they existed. But it was these pages that apparently had released me to write the book that earlier in 1978 had been awarded the Newbery Medal.

Here they are. Only the spelling and punctuation have been corrected.

> I am not sure I can tell this story. The pain is too fresh for it to fall into rational paragraphs, but I want to try. For David, for Lisa, for Lisa's mother, and for me.
>
> The small elementary school that my children attended was closed, and the students moved to a larger elementary school in the next neighborhood. Three of my four children adjusted quickly and happily into their new surroundings, but David, the second grader, was at sea. David is our third child, and since I was a third child too, I fancy I can understand the need to be special that seems to possess so many of us who will never be as handsome or clever or as magically old as our brothers and sisters who precede us. When he was three, David was torn between growing up to become a moon monster or a jellyfish, but soon after, he put away childish things and devoted himself to art. It was his art that made him special, so when he came home from the new school to report that "everyone" thought his pictures were "stupid," it was with the classic despair of the misunderstood genius. It was only the compulsory education law that persuaded me to return him to what he perceived to be an insensitive wasteland. It was a grim autumn for him—grim, that is, until he and Lisa found each other.
>
> Here I am very hazy as to the details. It may well be that David's perceptive young teacher saw the child's loneliness and hit upon a plan to relieve it. Or it may have been more like the classic tale—the smile across the crowded

room—that brought Lisa catapulting into our lives. I only know that one day David said solemnly, "Me and Lisa Hill are making a diorama about *Little House in the Big Woods,*" and from then on David was special again.

I'm trying to remember if it worried me that David had chosen a girl to be his best friend. I hope not, but I can't promise. At any rate, Lisa was the Liberation Movement's dream of the ideal girl. Bright, joy-filled, self-assured—the only girl to invade the second- and third-grade T-ball team. But sharing David's love for animals and art.

"It's your *girl* friend, David," his older brother would say, but David would take the phone unperturbed. Girl friends were a classification for the ones who chased you on the playground, hoping to grab you and kiss you. Lisa was no more a "girl friend" than Rose Kennedy is a Playboy bunny.

Lisa was the person you did everything with and told everything to. She laughed at his jokes (the ones his older brother and sister groaned over), and he laughed at hers. They played long, imaginative games in the woods behind her house, and in the late spring they both turned eight years old.

On a bright August afternoon, the phone call came. I listened in disbelief and horror and then quickly bypassed David, reading in the living room, to search out his father. Lisa was dead. Killed by lightning on a summer afternoon.

Somehow I told David and held him while he cried. Knowing in my heart that those tears would be only the first stirrings of a pain that would shake his whole young being.

We took him to the memorial service. He rather resented the two rows of Brownie Scouts. Was he not Lisa's best friend? So he made himself special by drawing a picture, "A funny one, so I won't make her sad," to give to Lisa's mother after the service.

School began, and with it the real work of grief. Other

children, uncomfortable with the unaccustomed intrusion of death, teased David. "You're in love with a dead girl," they'd say. And how could he deny it?

He told me later that he tried to cut them out by pretending Lisa were still there. "Lisa and me used to sit in the corner in music class and sing 'Free to be You and Me' real loud. So I sat there and tried to hear her voice, but there wasn't anybody there. I was all alone." He was sobbing, and so was I.

How can you comfort? We tried, by listening mostly. The school tried. The principal and his new teacher gave him special tasks and assignments calling for his artistic talents. They tried to be patient with his daydreaming and not remind him that last year he had been thus and so.

He kept thinking she would come back. And he would listen for her and watch for her. And then, when the hard truth began to dawn, he began to search within himself the reason for her death.

"I know why Lisa died," he said one night after his prayers. "It's because God hates me. Probably he's going to kill Mary next." (Mary is his beloved younger sister.)

Again, how does one comfort and reassure?

Lisa's mother has tried. She invited several of Lisa's friends to plant the bulbs she and Lisa had ordered together. And when she and David meet, she never fails to give him that assurance of his specialness that Lisa once provided. Lisa's grandmother made it possible for David to have pottery lessons. And perhaps of all the things we tried to do, this physical struggling with the clay was the most healing for him.

But he is not fully healed. Perhaps he will never be, and I am beginning to believe that this is right. How many people in their whole lifetimes have a friend who is to them what Lisa was to David? When you have had such a gift, should you ever forget it? Of course he will forget a little. Even now he is making other friendships. His life will go on, though hers could not. And selfishly I want his pain to ease. But how can I say that I want him to "get over it," as though having loved and been loved were some sort of disease? I want the joy of knowing Lisa and the sorrow of losing her to be a part of him and to shape him into growing levels of caring and understanding, perhaps as an artist, but certainly as a person.

UP FROM ELSIE DINSMORE

Pat! Pat! Pat!
There is the cat.
Where is the rat?
Pat, pat, pat.

As well as I can determine, this is my first published work. It appeared in the *Shanghai American,* our school newspaper, when I was seven years old. I cannot believe that any teacher or any parent, however doting, having read my early works, would have singled me out for a literary career.

From such primitive beginnings, I progressed by the age of eight to imitations of Elsie Dinsmore. Elsie, for those of you fortunate enough never to have been exposed to her, was a pious Victorian child whose mother was dead and whose father was an unfeeling unbeliever. The scene in *Elsie Dinsmore* that remains with me forever is the one in which Elsie's father commands her to play the piano for some of his friends. But, alas, it is Sunday, and Elsie's religious code prohibits her from such frivolity on the Sabbath. Imagine the moral dilemma—one commandment demands that she honor her father, the other demands that she keep the Sabbath. Elsie sits on the piano stool unwilling to play and yet forbidden to leave until she obeys. At last, she swoons to the floor. By fainting she brings her stern father to his knees in penitence. He realizes his great love for his beautiful and angelic child, and Elsie lives happily ever after through interminable sequels. Mrs. Finley, who knew a good thing when she had one, took little Elsie straight through to saintly grandmotherhood.

Imagine, if you can without damaging the mind, imitations of Elsie Dinsmore written by an eight-year-old. Compared to these early prose efforts, "Pat! Pat! Pat!" was a literary gem.

When she felt I might be getting a little uppity the other day, a friend suggested that I had not yet written *War and Peace*. And though I must readily concede that indeed I have not, still, looking back on those early days, I can't help the feeling that I've come, as the saying goes, a long way, baby. And yet, the child I was is not a different person from the woman I have become. That pious little hellion with delusions of grandeur still lives, and I am sure that what I write today is both for her and because of her.

Among the more than twice-told tales in my family is the tragic one about the year we lived in Richmond, Virginia, when I came home from first grade on February 14 without a single valentine. My mother grieved over this event until her death, asking me once why I didn't write a story about the time I didn't get any valentines. "But, Mother," I said, "*all* my stories are about the time I didn't get any valentines."

When people ask me what qualifies me to be a writer for children, I say I was once a child. But I was not only a child, I was, better still, a weird little kid, and though I would never choose to give my own children this particular preparation for life, there are few things, apparently, more helpful to a writer than having once been a weird little kid.

An earnest mother asked me last year how she could encourage her son to become a writer. I couldn't imagine what to say in reply. Have him born in a foreign country, start a war that drives him, not once, but twice like a refugee to another land, where his clothes, his speech, his very thoughts will cut him off from his peers; then, perhaps, he will begin to read books for comfort and invent elaborate fantasies inside his head for entertainment. You will be glad to know that I kept my mouth shut. I do not believe for one minute that her son needs to experience what I've experienced in order to write books. I'm sure there are plenty of fine writers who have overcome the disadvantages of a normal childhood and have gone on to do great things. It's just that we weird little kids do seem to have a head start.

When I enrolled in the Calvin H. Wiley School in Winston-Salem, North Carolina, I was nine years old, small for my age, and unbelievably timid. I had only recently gotten off a boat that had brought us refugeeing from China. I spoke English with a British accent and wore clothes out of a missionary barrel. Because children are somewhat vague about geography, my classmates knew only that I had come from somewhere over there and decided I was, if not a Japanese spy, certainly suspect, so they called me, in the friendly way that children have, "Jap." The only thing I could do anything about was the accent. Although I have since that time lived in five states and one foreign country, I still speak like a North Carolinian.

My accent is not the only thing I owe to Calvin H. Wiley

School. The school stood "on a hill above a meadow," as the school song had it, and on the hills and playgrounds of Wiley School were spent some of the most miserable hours of my life. When I read about children who had to pay protection money in the blackboard jungles of today, my thoughts fly back fondly to Pansy and her gang of seventh-grade Amazons who used to roam the playground, "seeking whom they might devour." I suppose they regarded me as a bit of delicious fun. On the other hand, I couldn't have been much of a challenge. They never had to lay a finger on me. I could spot them coming across the entire width of the school grounds and would be reduced to jelly on the spot.

I can't remember at what point I discovered the library. But I do not think it would be hyperbolic to say that it saved my sanity. That's where, of course, I first heard of the Newbery Medal, for I read everything of Kate Seredy and Robert Lawson and Rachel Fields that the shelves contained. And daydreamer that I was, it never occurred to me that someday there would be a book bearing that wonderful gold seal which would have my name on its cover.

I wish the librarian at Wiley School could know, but even if she is still alive, she's not likely to remember me. I was just one of her library aides. We shelved the books and read stories to the younger classes. I don't remember her name. I remember her manner, which was cheerful and precise. As I got to the sixth or seventh grade I was arranging cards in the card catalog, opening the new books, carefully, a bit at a time and gently pressing back the pages, pasting the pockets in the back. I was, before I left, even allowed to mend books. Do librarians mend books anymore? I hope so. What a loving, caring task. And even though I cannot remember her name or her face, I do remember how the librarian taught me to put on the double cloth binding, dipping the brush into the large pot of glue, pulling it against the edge of the pot, first one side of the brush, then the other, so that no errant drops would remain to fall upon the precious book. Years later it is a scene that found its way transformed into the opening pages of *The Master Puppeteer*. I still marvel at this woman, as fastidious as she was, entrusting us children with the care of her books. I have never taken more pride in any job I have held than I took in being a library aide at Calvin H. Wiley School. And I am sure that my sensuous love for books as paper, ink, and binding, treasures to be respected and cherished, is in large part due to the Wiley School librarian.

The Wiley School library, however, is not where my love of books began. That is a primal emotion tied up with the comforting lavender smell of my mother as I pressed my body as close as I could to hers and thrilled with horror at the idea of James James Morrison Morrison Weatherby, George Dupree's delinquent parent, who went casually strolling off to the end of the town and has never been heard of since. "Now you must know and understand, O Best Beloved. . . ." I suppose I am one of the few people in the world who hears Kipling in a soft Georgia accent. We didn't have many books when I was little. There were no libraries or bookstores with English books in Hwaianfu, China. But the books we had my mother read to us over and over. There was *Jo Boy*. I've never met anyone outside my family who has ever heard of *Jo Boy*. But the reason I don't kill spiders is because of *Jo Boy*—that goes for sweeping down cobwebs, too, in case some acquaintance thinks it's poor housekeeping. I can almost recite from heart the poems and stories of A. A. Milne, and I loved *The Wind in the Willows* almost as fanatically as the youth of the sixties loved Tolkien.

Then there was *The Secret Garden,* which was more a mystical experience than a book. For years I wanted to read it aloud to my own children and was terrified to. Suppose it would be Victorian mishmash, and they'd hate it, and I would be forced to hate it, too. But the age of miracles is not past. Despite all the gingerbread, it lives. The magic endures. And whenever I think that children don't like descriptive passages, I remember the smell and feel of the spring earth in the garden as Colin and Mary dug about the bulbs.

Of course, there was Elsie Dinsmore, too. She must have been in the school library in Shanghai, for I read those books myself. Don't blame my mother for Elsie Dinsmore. My mother had better taste. And being the pseudo pious child that I was, I listened to endless stories from the fat Egermeier's Bible Story book, but when I read myself, it was directly from the King James Bible. At school, at least for the first five years, I was usually terrified and therefore very quiet. People call that kind of child "good." At home I was so naughty that I felt I had to strike some kind of bargain with God or risk the fires of hell. I read the Bible and said a lot of prayers. And the lovely thing about doing good things for the wrong reason is that very often you get paid anyway. Never, of course, in the way you think you've earned, but in a better way. The word for this is "grace." So although I cannot help but poke fun at her—this comically solemn child who went from a well-deserved spanking to weep over the pages of her Bible thinking to earn a little on the credit side in the Book of Life—still it got me through the Bible several times and through certain parts of the Bible many times. It's the best education I ever had, and I'm very grateful to have had it early, even if the reason for it was less than theologically pure.

A horrible thought just struck me. I probably got the idea of reading the Bible through from Elsie Dinsmore. Wouldn't it be awful if I owed Elsie Dinsmore a debt as well as one to that funny child who read her? Maybe that's what humility consists of—the ability to acknowledge a debt to a source you are inclined to sneer at. I'm not that humble yet.

There are others to whom I joyfully acknowledge debt. Marjorie Kinnan Rawlings, for example. Back in the days when *The Yearling* was a Pulitzer Prize–winning adult novel, my mother went off on a trip. I don't know what she brought home to my brother and sisters, but I was eleven and she brought me a copy of *The Yearling.* Whether it was because my mother had given it to me in a way that complimented my intelligence and ability to understand or whether it was simply the power of this wonderful book alone, *The Yearling* immediately rose to the position of "the best book I've ever read." I don't believe that it is any accident that when I began to write a book that I knew would shake my foundations, the chief character was a lonely Southern country boy.

I feel like an archaeologist, as I try to reconstruct the books that shaped me—so much remains buried. How could I forget to mention Beatrix Potter, who was read to me, or Andersen or Grimm or *East o' the Sun and West o' the Moon,* of which the title alone sends a chill through me like a cold spring wind? I must have been in high school before I read *Mistress Masham's Repose.* It wasn't printed until 1946, but I remember it as a mind-stirring book of my childhood. I don't think I read much in high school. I do remember Dickens from that period and *The Scarlet Pimpernel* as a young teenager. In college I discovered Gerard Manley Hopkins and John Donne and made friends with Shakespeare and Sophocles. The Narnia books were being published then, and I lost my voice reading *The Lion, the Witch and the Wardrobe* aloud on the tour bus that was taking the college choir to Atlanta to sing.

The list is not endless. I have read far more since I left school than I ever did in school. There are great gaps in my literary education that I am still filling. The only problem with writing as a job is that it interferes with my reading. It is impossible for me to conceive of life without books. There are days when I don't have time to market or write or clean or even to eat lunch, but there always seems to be at least a little time to read. I cannot prove that all my reading makes me a better writer, though looking back at my early work I find a strong argument in its behalf. I am convinced that reading makes me a person richer in experience and compassion. And although, again, there is no objective proof, I believe that the reading of fiction has helped me not only to come to terms with the weird little kid I was and am but also to realize that almost everyone I meet has a weird little kid tucked away inside.

If then, after nearly forty years I have made peace with that child within myself, if with age and growth my life is far simpler and happier than it was at Wiley School, why am I still writing stories of outcast, terribly burdened children? People always want to know when I'm going to write a story with a happy ending. One librarian gave it to me straight. "Every time I start one of your books I try to figure out how you're going to ruin the ending this time." Why do I continue to inflict my own grief and sin on innocent children? Can't I allow the young a few short years free of the cares of human experience as we adults must know them?

The answer, sadly, is no. I sat, as many of you must have, with my children one afternoon and evening before the television set and watched over and over again a film that showed the

President of our nation being shot. My children have grown up in the shadow of the death of a President, in an era of increasing terrorism and senseless war. They discuss the possibilities of nuclear obliteration at the supper table. They have never known real hunger, but they are quite aware how hungry most of the world is. They know exactly how many black children are dead or missing in Atlanta. Two of them have had close friends of their own age die, and all of them have known their beloved grandmother's death from cancer. The older boy was discussing with the others last week whether he should seek in another year or so to become a conscientious objector or register to fight in future Viet Nams. Tucked among the cosmic terrors are math tests and relations to the opposite sex and party-night pimples. Even, you see, the most fortunate of our youth are far from carefree, and most children in this world have never known that state of innocence which some romantic adults persist in linking to childhood.

This is why children have always loved the tough old stories of myth and fairy tale and the unexpurgated Bible. They have not had the words or experience to explain it, but they have known in their deepest selves that though truth is seldom comfortable, it is, finally, the strongest comfort.

I do not pretend, nor do I know any writers who do, to have a monopoly on Truth. I can only see the human experience through the one pair of eyes I have been given. I can only tell the truth as I, with all my sins and limitations, can apprehend it. But I promise you I do not have two truths, one for adults and another for children. I write about the difficulties of the human experience with hope, not because I think a writer should tack on a hopeful message for young readers, but because despite all the contrary evidence, I am a person who lives in hope. That is how I see the world, and that is how, therefore, I must write about it.

It has been a long journey for me from Elsie Dinsmore swooning in piety off the piano bench to Louise Bradshaw shaking her fist in the face of God, and some of you may well ask if the direction has always been upward. I can't decide the answer for you. I must simply do what I can. And yet, when a seventh-grade girl whom I have never seen before and whose name I will never know waits until all her classmates are out of earshot and then whispers to me, "I loved *Jacob Have I Loved*," the weird little kid inside me reaches out to the child before me, and I am filled with joy. We understand each other. No writer could ask for more.

NATIONAL BOOK AWARD ACCEPTANCE

❧

THE MASTER PUPPETEER
1977

People ask me why I write for children. I don't write for children, I say, I write for myself, and then look in the catalog to see how old I am. But it's not true that I simply write for myself. I do write for children. For my own four children and for others who are faced with the question of whether they dare to become adult, responsible for their own lives and the lives of others. They remind me of the Biblical children of Israel, trembling on the bank of the Jordan. You'll remember that Moses sent spies ahead, who came back to tell of the richness of the land. But ten of the spies advised the Israelites to turn back. The cities are fortified, they said, and the people are giants. It would be better to return to slavery in Egypt or to wander aimlessly in the desert.

I want to become a spy like Joshua and Caleb. I have crossed the river and tangled with a few giants, but I want to go back and say to those who are hesitating, Don't be afraid to cross over. The promised land is worth possessing, and we are not alone. I want to be a spy for hope.

NATIONAL BOOK AWARD ACCEPTANCE

❦

THE GREAT GILLY HOPKINS
1979

I wrote this book because, by chance rather than by design, I was for two months a foster mother. Now, as a mother I am not a finalist for any prizes, but on the whole I'm serviceable. I was not serviceable as a foster mother, and this is why: I knew from the beginning that the children were going to be with us only a short time, so when a problem arose, as problems will, I'd say to myself, "I can't really deal with that. They'll be here only a few weeks." Suddenly and too late I heard what I had been saying. I was regarding two human beings as Kleenex, disposable. And it forced me to think, what must it be like for those thousands upon thousands of children in our midst who find themselves rated disposable? So I wrote a book, a confession of sin, in which one of these embittered children meets the world's greatest foster mother. Virginia Buckley said that my characters were mythic; a critic being less kind used the word unbelievable. I knew when I wrote the book that Gilly and Trotter were larger than life. I did it deliberately, to get attention, like that unknown lover who wrote across the underpass near our house in letters ten feet high, "I love you, Grace Kowaski."

But the wonderful thing about being a writer is that it gives you readers, readers who bring their own stories to the story you have written, people who have the power to take your mythic, unbelievable, ten-foot-high characters and fit them to the shape of their own lives.

From THE HORN BOOK
(August 1979)

FROM THE

NEWBERY MEDAL ACCEPTANCE

BRIDGE TO TERABITHIA

1978

The summer our son David was three years old he fell in love with bridges. I understood just how he felt, being a lover of bridges myself, and coming home from Lake George the whole family took delight in the bridges along the way. We were spending the night with our Long Island cousins; it was well after dark, and everyone was getting cranky by the time the last bridge was crossed.

"When is the next bridge, Mommy?" David asked.

"There aren't any more," I told him. "We're almost at Uncle Arthur's house now."

"Just one more bridge, Mommy, please, just one more bridge," he said, believing in his three-year-old heart that mothers can do anything, including instant bridge building.

"There aren't any more bridges, sweetheart, we're almost there."

He began to weep. *"Please*, Mommy, just one more bridge."

Nothing we said could console him. I was at my wit's end. Why couldn't he understand that I was not maliciously with-holding his heart's desire—that there was no way I could conjure up a bridge and throw it in the path of our car? When would he know that I was a human being, devoid of any magic power?

It was later that night that I remembered. The next day I could give him a bridge, and not just any bridge. The next day I could give him the Verrazano Bridge. I could hardly wait.

That is the last and only time I was given credit for building the Verrazano Bridge, but it occurs to me that I have spent a good part of my life trying to construct bridges. Usually my bridges have turned out looking much more like the bridge of Terabithia, a few planks over a nearly dry gully, than like that elegant span across the Narrows. There were so many chasms I saw that needed bridging—chasms of time and culture and disparate human nature—that I began sawing and hammering at the rough wood planks for my children and for any other children who might read what I had written.

But of course I could not make a bridge for them any more than I could conjure one up that night on Long Island. I discovered gradually and not without a little pain that you don't put together a bridge for a child. You become one—you lay yourself across the chasm.

It is there in the Simon and Garfunkel song—

> *Like a bridge over troubled water*
> *I will lay me down . . .*

The waters to be crossed are not always troubled. The land on the other side of the river may be flowing with joy, not to mention milk and honey. But still the bridge that the child trusts or delights in—and, in my case, the book that will take children from where they are to where they might be—needs to be made not from synthetic or inanimate objects, but from the stuff of life. And a writer has no life to give but her own.

* * *

Theodore Gill has said, "The artist is the one who gives form to difficult visions." This statement comes alive for me when I pore over Peter Spier's *Noah's Ark*. The difficult vision is not the destruction of the world. We've had too much practice imagining that. The difficult vision that Mr. Spier has given form to is that in the midst of this destruction, as well as beyond it, there are life and humor and caring, along with a lot of manure shoveling. For me those final few words "and he planted a vineyard" ring with the same joy as "he found his supper waiting for him and it was still hot."

In talking with children who have read *Bridge to Terabithia*, I have met several who do not like the ending. They resent the fact that Jesse would build a bridge into the secret kingdom that he and Leslie had shared. The thought of May Belle following in the footsteps of Leslie is bad enough, but the hint that the thumb-sucking Joyce Ann may come as well is totally abhorrent to these readers. How could I allow Jesse to build a bridge for the unworthy? they ask me. Their sense of what is fitting and right and just is offended. I hear my young critics out and do not try to argue with them, for I know as well as they do that May Belle is not Leslie, nor will she ever be. But perhaps someday they will understand Jesse's bridge as an act of grace, which he built not because of who May Belle was, but because of who he

From the Newbery Medal Acceptance, 1978

himself had become crossing the gully into Terabithia. I allowed him to build the bridge because I dare to believe with the prophet Hosea that the very valley where evil and despair defeat us can become a gate of hope—if there is a bridge.

In closing, I want to explain the Japanese word on the dedication page of *Bridge to Terabithia*. The word is *banzai*, which some of you will remember from old war movies. I am very annoyed when writers throw in Italian and German phrases that I cannot understand, but suddenly as I wrote the dedication to this book, *banzai* seemed to be the only word I knew that was appropriate. The two characters that make up the word say, "All years," but the word itself combines the meanings of our English word *Hurrah* with the ancient salute to royalty, "Live forever!" It is a cry of triumph and joy, a word full of hope in the midst of the world's contrary evidence. It is the word I wanted to say through *Bridge to Terabithia*. It is a word that I think Leslie Burke would have liked. It is my salute to all of you whose lives are bridges for the young.

Banzai!

From THE HORN BOOK
(August 1978)

NEWBERY MEDAL ACCEPTANCE

❦

JACOB HAVE I LOVED
1981

I was thrilled, honored, gratified, not to say shocked to learn that *Jacob Have I Loved* was to be given the 1981 Newbery Medal. But there was a problem. "What shall I say in San Francisco?" I cried out to my husband. "I don't know what to say." He proposed: "Thank you." Yes, but what next? A writer I know suggested that it was time I said to the American Library Association: "We have got to stop meeting like this." I was sorely tempted, but these speeches tend to get preserved, and who wants to appear flippant to posterity? I complained to another friend that everything I thought of sounded either coy or dumb, and she replied: "Well, I don't think you need to worry about coy. It's just not your style to be coy." It took me several seconds to get it. Call Purnell would have caught on sooner. Into the midst of all this inner turmoil there came one cool, clear voice. It had a distinct Chesapeake Bay island ring to it. "Oh, my blessed. Wouldn't you know? Here I bring up a prize catch and the fool's fixing to ruin it for me."

So with Sara Louise Bradshaw prodding me at the end of her skiff pole, I was made to turn from the frazzled writer to the book. How could I forget that it is books that are being honored, books for children? And who could be happier than I to join in the sixtieth anniversary of such a celebration? This speech, then, must be concerned not with me but with Jacob, whom I have loved off and on for years.

Whenever I speak, one of the questions sure to be asked during the question-and-answer time is: "How long does it take to write a book?" as though books, like elephants or kittens, had a regular and therefore predictable gestation period. Often I will begin my reply by asking, "Which book?" trying to indicate that each book is different and has its own unique history. There is, however, one answer that would be true in every case, but whenever I try to put it in words I find myself swimming in pomposity. The correct answer, you see, is this: It has taken all my life to write this book. Maybe longer.

The conflict at the core of *Jacob Have I Loved* began east of Eden, in the earliest stories of my heritage. Cain was jealous of his brother, and, we are told, "Cain rose up against Abel his brother and slew him." If, in our Freudian orientation, we speak of the basic conflict as that between parent and child, the Bible, which is the earth from which I spring, is much more concerned with the relationships among brothers and sisters. "A friend loveth at all times," says the writer of Proverbs, "but a brother is born for adversity." They never taught us the second half of that verse in Sunday School.

The fairy tales, too, are full of the youngest brother or sister who must surpass his supposedly more clever elders or outwit the wicked ones. In *The Uses of Enchantment* Bruno Bettelheim suggests that a great deal of the apparent rivalry between

117

brothers and sisters in fairy tales is in actuality an Oedipal conflict, since the usual number of brothers or sisters is three. In the stories of two brothers or sisters, Bettelheim suggests that the story is about the divided self, which must be integrated before maturity can be attained. Although both of these explanations make sense, I do not think that we can avoid the most obvious meaning of the stories, which is that among children who grow up together in a family there run depths of feeling that will permeate their souls for both good and ill as long as they live.

I was the middle child of five, swivel position, the youngest of the three older children and the oldest of the three younger. Although I can remember distinctly occasions when I determined that someday I would show my older brother and sister a thing or two, and I have no recollection that my two younger sisters were plotting to do me in, still the stories in which the younger by meanness or magic or heavenly intervention bested the elder always bothered me. They simply weren't fair. The divine powers, whether the Hebrew God or the European fairy, always weighted the contest. And although the civilized Calvinist part of my nature spoke in quiet tones about the mystery of divine election, there was a primitive, beastly part, a Caliban, that roared out against such monstrous injustice. Novels, I have learned, tend to come out of the struggle with the untamed beast.

It was the fall of 1977. *The Great Gilly Hopkins* was at the printers, the hoopla following the National Book Award for *The Master Puppeteer* was over, and I had finished the curriculum unit on the Shang and Chou Dynasties of ancient China. I could no longer put it off. I must face the beast in its den, or, what was worse, that stack of blank paper beside my typewriter.

How do you begin a book? People always want to know how you begin. If only I knew. Think of all the agonizing days and weeks I could have spared myself, not to mention my long-suffering family. They know better than to ask me about my work when I'm trying to start all over again. My replies are never gracious. There must be a better way. My way is to write whatever I can, hoping against hope that, with all the priming, the pump will begin to flow once more.

Here is a sample from those dry, dry days in the fall of 1977:

> Her name is Rachel Ellison but I don't know yet where she lives. It might be in the city or in the country. It might even be Japan. It seems important to know what her parents do. How does religion come into the story? Will Rachel be burdened by guilt as well as everything else? Will her relationship to God play counterpoint to her relationship to her brother? I said brother but perhaps after all it has to be a sister. I'm avoiding sister because it comes too close to home. Am I contemplating a book I can't write? The feelings start boiling up everytime I begin to think about it. All raw feeling. No story. There has to be a story. There has to be a setting. There has to be something more than boiling anger. Why am I angry? . . . Where is the key that turns this into a book? Jacob and Esau. Cain and Abel. Rachel and Leah. Prodigal and elder brother. Joseph and his brothers. The sons of David. Lord, make my brother give me the portion of the inheritance that comes to me. Maybe Rachel's brother is an adopted South Asian war orphan. Sister.
>
> Excitement to pity to rage to hatred to some kind of accommodation. Step one: Go to the library and find out everything possible about Southeast Asian orphans. . . .

And I was off on a wild-goose chase that lasted for days.

All November and December were spent in pursuit of similar

geese. How long this would have gone on I have no way of knowing, but Christmas came and with it a gift of grace. It was not even intended as a gift for me. My sister Helen gave our son John a copy of William Warner's *Beautiful Swimmers: Watermen, Crabs, and the Chesapeake Bay*. I began reading it during those low after-Christmas days, and by the time the new year dawned I had a place to set my story, the Chesapeake Bay, less than an hour from my front door.

In the Bay there are many islands, most of which are not inhabited. Two of them, Smith and Tangier islands, are separated by miles of water from the rest of America. Even now, with television, telephones, and, in the case of Tangier, an airstrip, they seem a world apart. My story was going to be chiefly about a young adolescent who felt terribly isolated. Of course, all fourteen-year-olds who are not social clones feel isolated, but what better way to show this isolation than an island? Rass (the name for my island squirted up from my subconscious and has yet to reveal its source or meaning), Rass would be none of the actual islands, but something like all of them.

Now I began going to the library as well as to the Bay to find out everything I could about the Chesapeake. At the same time I began setting down on scraps of paper and three-by-five cards ideas as they would occur, things that might happen in the story.

What about a grandmother or other live-in relative who spouts pietisms? She may be one who brings up "Jacob have I loved . . ." theme.

Old man gets off ferry. He left thirty years before and has come back. Takes shack at farthest end of island to live as recluse.

Make the kid sentimental—moons over tombstones—
tries to convert friend who is boy to sentimentality.

These are bound with the same sturdy rubber band that holds
notes taken from reading and observation.

pain of being stung in the eye by jellyfish

how peelers are separated
   2 wks. to go—snots, greens, white sign crabs
   1 wk—pink sign
   hrs to go before busting—rank, red sign

reactions to thunderstorms
   chopped down mast
   climbing up it swinging hatchet at the almighty—
     daring God to meet him halfway—

cats around garbage dump scavenging. Big cats.

wintering birds on Smith
"Oh, my blessed, what a noise."

There is another large pack of four-by-six cards, but I think all
those notes were collected much later. I think so, not that I ever
seem capable of dating, but the cards are ones I remember
buying at Gray's Pharmacy in Norfolk. So between the first
batch of cards and the second, there came the January 1978
announcement of a Newbery Medal, the acceptance, the knowledge that after thirteen years in Takoma Park we would be
moving, the discovery of my mother's terminal cancer, the
choice of *Gilly* as the Newbery Honor Book, the move to
Norfolk, Mother's death, and a National Book Award. That is
not everything that happened in our lives between the fall of

1977 and the spring of 1979, but it may give you some idea why poor *Jacob* was languishing.

But even as I present to you these impeccable excuses, I know in my heart that the reason I nearly despaired of finishing this book was more the internal storms it stirred up than those that came from without. I was trying to write a story that made my stomach churn every time I sat down at the typewriter. "Love is strong as death," says the writer of the Song of Songs, "jealousy is cruel as the grave." I did not want ever again to walk the dark path into that cruelty.

Yet even while I was having trouble going back into my young self, I was being drawn more and more into the world of the book. I knew that in Rass I was trying to create a facsimile of the Bay islands, but my feeling as I worked was not so much that of a creator as that of an explorer. Here was a hidden world that it was my task to discover. If I failed, this world would remain forever unknown.

I do not mean by this that I thought I had a monopoly on the Chesapeake Bay. Not long after I had begun work on my book, James Michener's massive *Chesapeake* was published. I read it with dread, fearing that he might have preempted me, might have discovered my world. But he hadn't. He couldn't have. The Chesapeake world I was exploring was mine alone. No other living soul had access to it unless I could somehow reveal it in *Jacob*. I think I have finally learned that no one can steal your novel from you. No matter how closely his material may come to yours, he can only write his story, and you, yours—the intricate design of an individual life upon some portion of the outside world. I knew, for better or worse, that if I did not write *Jacob*, it would never be written.

I say my world, my story, but it hardly ever felt like mine. For one thing, it refused to obey my rules. I have always sworn that I would never write a book in the first person. It is too limiting, too egotistical. And yet, the book refused any voice but Louise's. "Oh, well," I said to myself, "I'd better get it down any way I can in the first draft. In the next draft I can write it properly."

At some point I wrote a very peculiar note to myself. Not content with writing a book in first person, I apparently was thinking of writing it as three first-person stories—one for Louise, one for Caroline, and one for Call. "Perhaps," I added, "end with a fourth section which goes back to Sara Louise and ties the story together."

Heavens above. I think the only reason this book ever got written is that I would regularly lose all my notes. I must remember that next time. Take all the notes you wish, but do not fail to lose them once you start.

By now it was the fall of 1979. I was piling page upon page, revision upon revision, until finally my husband made a strong suggestion that it was time to get the manuscript out of the house and to Virginia Buckley. I think he felt that if drastic steps were not taken soon, he would be living with *Jacob* in an eternal triangle. He was right. I had become so entangled in the story that I did not know if it was worth further effort, if it would ever be a publishable book. So I sent it.

Virginia got it on Friday and called me on Sunday. "I love it," she said. I knew that she did not mean it was perfect. I knew there were months of intensive rewriting ahead, but you cannot imagine the joy with which I heard those words. I know very well that I am capable of writing a bad book, but I have never, in my right mind, believed that Virginia would publish one. She loved *Jacob,* and, as I began the painstaking revisions, I came to love it, too—until, though I never managed to bring it to perfection, I felt that it was the best that I could do. My child had grown up and must, at long last, be let go.

An earnest young reporter asked me: "What are you trying to do when you write for children?" "I'm trying to write as well as I possibly can," I answered. He thought I hadn't understood his question. "No, no," he said. "What I mean is, what is your philosophy of writing for children? Isn't there some moral you want to get across to them? Aren't there some values you wish to instill in your young readers?" "I'm trying," I said, "to write for my readers the best story, the truest story of which I am capable." He gave up on me and changed the subject, frustrated and annoyed. He seemed to share the view of many intelligent, well-educated, well-meaning people that, while adult literature may aim to be art, the object of children's books is to whip the little rascals into shape.

But you and I know better. We know that those of us who write for children are called, not to do something to a child, but to be someone for a child. "Art," in Frances Clarke Sayers' wonderfully passionate definition, is "a controlled fury of desire to share one's private revelation of life." And she the librarian summons us who are writers to the service of art—to give the best that is in us to "the audience that lives by what it feeds upon."

Among my notes I found this one written while I was stalled one day during August of 1979. I can date it because it is written on Gene Namovicz's electric typewriter and is full of stray *l*'s and *k*'s.

There is another sibling rivalry in the story of Jacob. It is, of course, the story of Leah and Rachel. "Jacob have I loved—" Poor Leah, the homely elder sister. Married in trickery to the man passionately in love with her younger

From the Newbery Medal Acceptance, 1981

sister. She goes to his bed and must lie there and bear his
seeing who she is. Watch his face as the truth of his
father-in-law's treachery dawns. His disappointment.
How does he react? What does he say? Even if, and it is
hard to believe he might have been, even if in his own
disappointment he remembers her pain and tries to be
tactful and kind, that very kindness would be next to
unbearable, if Leah loves him at all. Esau's grief is nothing
compared to Leah's. She must watch her husband go
joyfully to her sister and joylessly come to her. But God
does give her many sons. That would be a comfort if we
did not know that Rachel, who only has two sons, is the
mother of Joseph—that younger brother of all younger
brothers. This puts a new dimension into the phrase,
"Jacob have I loved . . ." It is a woman speaking now, a
wronged and grieving woman, not God. The loving is not
here a matter of divine election but of the eternal weight of
women who have neither the beauty of Rachel nor the
cleverness of Rebekkah. What shall we do for the Leahs?

The only thing I can do for the Leahs, the Esaus, and the
Louises, is to give them now, while they are young, the best, the
truest story of which I am capable. I have learned, for all my
failings and limitations, that when I am willing to give myself
away in a book, readers will respond by giving themselves away
as well, and the book that I labored over so long becomes in our
mutual giving something far richer and more powerful than I
could have ever imagined. I thank you, and I thank God that I
have been allowed to take part in this miracle once again.

And now, if you will excuse me, I have this book I want to
write.

From THE HORN BOOK
(August 1981)

125

ABOUT THE AUTHOR

Katherine Paterson's works have received wide acclaim and been published in many languages. Among her books are *Park's Quest*; *Come Sing, Jimmy Jo*, an ALA Notable Children's Book; *Rebels of the Heavenly Kingdom*; and *Gates of Excellence*. Also, *Jacob Have I Loved* and *Bridge to Terabithia*, winners of the 1981 and 1978 Newbery Medals; *The Great Gilly Hopkins*, a Newbery Honor Book and winner of the 1979 National Book Award; and *The Master Puppeteer*, which received the 1977 National Book Award.

Katherine Paterson, the daughter of missionaries, was born in China and spent her early childhood there. Educated in both China and the United States, she was graduated from King College in Bristol, Tennessee, and later received master's degrees from the Presbyterian School of Christian Education in Richmond, Virginia, and Union Theological Seminary in New York.

The parents of four children, Mrs. Paterson and her husband live in Barre, Vermont.

DATE DUE

AUG 4 2004			